A REAL MAN STANDS TALL

SAFE IN MY ARMS

JAMES A. HARRELL JR.

A REAL MAN STANDS TALL
SAFE IN MY ARMS

Scripture quotations are from the Holy Bible, King James Version (Authorized Version). First published in 1611. Quoted from the KJV Classic Reference Bible, Copyright © 1983 by The Zondervan Corporation.

iUniverse books may be ordered through booksellers or by contacting:

iUniverse
1663 Liberty Drive
Bloomington, IN 47403
www.iuniverse.com
1-800-Authors (1-800-288-4677)

ISBN: 978-1-4917-9980-2 (sc)
ISBN: 978-1-4917-9981-9 (e)

Library of Congress Control Number: 2016911035

Print information available on the last page.

iUniverse rev. date: 07/27/2016

DEDICATION

This book is dedicated to:

Brandon, Kahlelil, Derrick, Terrance, Joshua, Caleb, Rueben, Nicholas,

Shawn, Jeremy, Deveckeo, Jaylen, Jerome, Li'l Alfred, Jarrin, Marcus,

Ke Jarrion, Mike, Roderick, Troy, Johnny Ray, Orlando, and Ramsey.

Because a boy is an adult, that doesn't make him a man. A boy is a man in training.

MY WISH LIST

I wish my father was…

My provider
My protector
My pastor
My counselor
My agent
My manager
My trainer
My coach
My best friend
My role model
My hero

FOOD FOR THOUGHT

Children love because of and in spite of – unconditional love.

I can close my eyes every night and sleep because you are my father.

I don't go to bed hungry at night because you are my father.

I depend on you because you are my father.

I look up to you because you are my father.

I believe in you because you are my father.

I trust you because you are my father.

I love you because you are my father.

Father, please don't let me down.

ACKNOWLEDGMENTS

To God be the glory for all the things He has done and has allowed to happen in my life. His Grace and Mercy encompass me. Without Him, I am nothing, and I can do nothing. I thank Him for the gifts of talents.

To my mother, Gloria Mae Richardson: You are my role model for life! Although you didn't teach me how to be a man, you have made me a better man. Your love and support have been my bedrock throughout my entire life. I love you!

In loving memory of Daniel Muse, Jr. I miss your smile. You were a gentle giant. Enjoy your rest.

In loving memory of Victor Muse. Thank you so very much for your contribution to this book, allowing me to interview you and witness your love and admiration for your father. You are a prince and we miss you. Sleep on and enjoy your rest.

In loving memory of my friend and brother, Edward Slocum. I wish you were here to see how high your big brother is soaring. I'm sorry that I never told you that I loved you and appreciated the blessing of your friendship. Your death has shown me that tomorrow is not promised to any of us. To die of a heart attack at the young age of twenty-two blows my mind! Sleep on little brother. I will see you again.

In loving memory of Lawrence "Goo" Harrison: Thank you for being my mentor during my storm seasons. You were my role model when I needed someone to believe in. I have much love and respect for you.

To Durund Elzey: I want to thank you for your friendship and brotherhood. The bible says that there is a friend that sticks closer than a brother. You are such a friend. I want you to know that I am proud of you. I also want to thank you and Durund II for posing for the cover of my book. D2, you are blessed to have a father like Durund.

To Elroy Jackson, my cousin: Thank you for your input and support on this project. Your tribute to your father (my uncle) is a great enhancement to this book. I love you, "cuz."

To Yvonne Collins, my cousin: Thank you for allowing me to interview you for my tribute to Uncle Leo, your father.

To Shemaiah Hill, my cousin: Thank you for taking the photo for the front cover of my book. Your gift will make room for you. You are a great photographer.

To George Zhou, my brother like no other from a different mother in Zimbabwe, Africa: Thank you for inspirations from the motherland. If God permits, I will see you soon.

To Reginald Warford, my cousin and brother: Thank you for your contribution to this project. I share your pain. Even though you are my cousin, I love you like a brother.

To Bishop Lester and Pastor Fran Love: Thank you for the soothing breezes of inspiration you blew into my life. Higher Heights and Deeper Depths are what I hear in my spirit.

To Alfred Raboteau, my brother from another mother: Although you are a bit rough around the edges, God has a plan for your life. He said He would make the crooked places straight and the rough smooth. Let go and let God and watch Him move in your life. I have much love for you, my brother.

To Reverend Daniel Muse, Sr., Missionary Bobbie Muse, Tony Muse, Margaret Muse Mitchell, and Victor Muse: I want to thank each of you for believing in me and my vision and allowing me to interview you for this project. Your family is blessed beyond measure. All of you have made a great contribution to my book. Thank you!

To Sharlotte "Tina" Turner, Pastor Elisa Edwards, Rev. Mark Square, Brenda Seals, Durund and Courtney Elzey (my focus group): Thank you all for reading my manuscript and offering your suggestions and comments. Your input has greatly enriched my book.

To my seed donors – Gloria Mae Richardson (mother), Reginald Warford (cousin), Brandon Wagner (Christian brother), and Attorney Tanzanika Ruffin (friend): God gives seed to the sower. Because of your seed sown, you have allowed my manuscript to blossom. I am eternally grateful and thankful. The best is yet to come. God is good all the time, and all the time God is good.

To Jerome Clark, my editor, thank you for your dedication and precision for details. Your thoughts have moved me to tears and your words have validated my ministry as a writer.

Finally, I want to thank everyone who has sown seeds of inspiration in my life. I also would like to thank all those individuals who have sown seeds of discord. I thank each of you for your help in cultivating my field. May God richly bless each of you, according to the seeds that you have sown.

CONTENTS

WINTER
INTERVIEWS

SPRING
ESSAYS

SUMMER
POEMS

FALL
LETTERS

PREFACE

While crossing Canal Street in downtown New Orleans on Wednesday morning, December 22, 1999, I was struck by a speeding car that had run a red light. The impact sent me soaring into the air. The driver fled the scene of the accident; it was a hit-and-run. I was later rushed to Charity Hospital where I underwent surgery for two fractured bones in my left leg. I survived both the accident and surgery. In February the following year, while resting on my sofa, I was inspired to write a poem entitled, *If I Were Your Man*. When I finished writing that poem, I was inspired to write another poem entitled, *If God Didn't Exist*. Once I finished it, I was inspired to write, yet, another poem entitled, *If I Were God*. In the span of about two hours, I had written three poems. That was very unusual for me, because I neither wrote nor liked poetry. I believed that the Spirit of the Lord was urging me to write. I wanted to be obedient, so I grabbed my crutches, a pen and some paper, and I went to my living room. I did this each morning. Once there, I reclined on my sofa, elevated my leg, and waited for inspiration. Poems began flowing from my soul like water out of a faucet. In less than two months, I had written an entire book of poetry. I was so amazed.

———⟡———

On the morning of May 24, 2000, I was putting my trash out. This was two weeks after God healed me from my first accident. Suddenly, I was struck by a drunk driver. He had lost control of his car. I suffered head injuries which included severe brain trauma. Once again, I was rushed to Charity Hospital. I was in a coma for nearly two weeks. When I came out of my coma, I was released and sent home. Unbeknown to me, my mother had moved me to her home back in Amite. Approximately one month after I was released from the hospital, I came to myself. I woke up from my sleep and noticed that, along with most of my belongings, I was at my mother's house. Dazed and confused, I asked my mother for an explanation. She informed me that I had been involved in another accident. She also said that the doctors didn't have much hope of me recovering. Death had been knocking at the door. But my mother had been too busy praying, interceding for my life, to answer it. There's no doubt in my mind that if it weren't for my praying, faithful, loving mother, I wouldn't be alive today.

Although I survived that accident and surgery, I was having problems with my short-term memory. Simply put, I was becoming senile. I wasn't willing to accept this. So I set out on a course to rectify it. I determined that the best action to take, to stimulate my memory and retrain my brain, was to indulge in reading and writing therapy. So each morning, I grabbed my bible, dictionary, pen and paper, went outside, sat down at my mother's picnic table, and started my therapy. When inspiration came to me, I wrote as I was prompted.

In two months I had written a second manuscript. At that moment, I had an epiphany. After each of my accidents, I wrote a manuscript. A full length book. When I graduated from high school, way back in 1983, I had aspirations of being a writer. But with the stress of just trying to make it from day to day, trying to maintain, that dream got shelved.

Prior to my first accident, I had not written anything in years. Now, after two accidents, I had written not one, but two books – one after each accident. It was clear to me that God wanted me to be a writer. The time had come for me to take my dream off the shelf, remove the cobwebs, and brush off the dust. My dream of being a writer was resurrected.

To show God that I had finally seen the light and didn't need a third accident to compel me to write, I came up with an idea for a third book. I began to write the first draft. And that first draft is this very book which you, dear reader, are now holding, and reading.

While writing, I visited various churches around the area, to give my testimony and to recite my poetry. My presentations were well received, if I must say so myself. On many occasions, I received standing ovations.

People seemed excited that a local young man like myself had written a book.

In February, 2001, seven months after I started writing therapy, I moved back into my apartment in New Orleans. I had two completed manuscripts and one was halfway complete. For the next few years, I was too busy to write. I guess my thoughts and ideas had to marinate.

On August 28, 2005, I was awakened from my sleep by a phone call. It was my friend and coworker, Al. He wanted to know where I was. Al and his family had evacuated to Atlanta, escaping the impending fury of Hurricane Katrina. I told him that I was going to ride out the storm in my apartment. I was in the lower 9th Ward. Al told me that I was stupid. He said he would keep in touch and continue to check on me to make sure that I was alright, then we said goodbye.

Minutes later, the phone rang again. It was my roommate, L.T. He too had called to check on me. L.T., his mom, and grandmother were on their way to Virginia. He asked me about my plans. Just like I told Al, I told L.T. that I would ride out the storm in our apartment. L.T. said that I was crazy. Not long after I hung up the phone with him, my phone rang yet again. This time it was my spiritual brother, Durund, calling to check in on me. He and his family had evacuated to Florida. Durund informed me that Louisiana Governor Kathleen Blanco had issued a mandatory evacuation for Orleans Parish and for the surrounding areas.

Durund also told me that the city and state police would be shutting down the highways and interstates in a matter of hours and that I wouldn't be able to leave if I had a change of heart. I decided to rethink my plans. After Durund told me how huge the storm was, I grabbed my car keys and walked out the door. I said to myself, I can replace books, clothes, furniture, and appliances, but I can't duplicate my manuscripts. I turned around and grabbed my book bag that contained my writings. Then I left. To be honest, I didn't believe that it would be as bad as everyone had feared. But in the event that I was wrong, I wouldn't be caught in New Orleans. I drove to my hometown, Amite, in bumper-to-bumper traffic. When I arrived, I immediately went to bed, and I slept through the night.

When I woke up the next day, there was no electricity or running water. There were so many downed trees and light poles. I was amazed that I slept through all that. As I listened to the news on my car radio, I was in total shock. Overnight, I became homeless and jobless. I could not believe what had happened to New Orleans. I had always taken pride in my being what I considered *the landlord of my soul*, which was my being in control of my own life.

As I listened to the news reports, I grew weary with each passing hour. Each day Al called to try to convince me to come to Atlanta. When I realized the fact that I wouldn't be returning home to New Orleans anytime soon, I started seriously considering moving to Atlanta. After much contemplation on my part and urging from Al, I decided to throw caution to the wind and move to Atlanta. Like so many other evacuees, a motel room became my temporary new home.

Over the next several weeks, I made numerous trips back home to see if I could salvage anything from my apartment and also to see the catastrophic effects of Katrina on my beloved city. Each time I tried to cross over the Industrial Canal and go into the lower 9th Ward, the National Guard wouldn't let me in. The lower 9th Ward was one of the areas which sustained the most damage.

In October, 2005, nearly two months after the storm struck, I learned that the authorities were allowing the residents of the lower 9th Ward to come back and check on their properties. Without hesitation, I drove back to New Orleans. What I thought would be only a one-day or two-day stay actually turned out to be seven weeks. When I arrived at my apartment, I saw what Katrina's fury had done to it. The locks were all corroded. In order to get in, I had to climb on a fence, push the air conditioning unit through the window unto the floor, then crawl through the window. Once inside, I proceeded with extreme caution. I was afraid that, besides mildew and bacteria, snakes may have slithered in. Judging from the water marks on the walls, the water had risen over seven feet.

As I scanned around the rooms, I was devastated at what I saw. Nothing could be salvaged. Nothing. Tears filled my eyes, however none of them fell. I considered this as the closure I needed in order to move on with my life. After I had seen all that I needed to see, I went out through the back door and drove through the 9th Ward, taking note of all the destruction. My eyes looked at pure devastation. Home was no longer home, and it wouldn't be home for many years to come.

Determined to return a sense of normalcy to my life, I drove back to

Atlanta and began looking for an apartment. In November, 2005, I moved into one. It was located in a place called Forest Park, just outside the city. Several months later, I decided to look over my manuscripts.

When I retrieved them from my book bag, I discovered that one of them was missing. I was frantic. The one I titled, *A Real Man Stands Tall*, was nowhere to be found. Had I unknowingly left it back at my apartment in New Orleans? If I had, could it have survived the effects of Hurricane Katrina? As I reflected on my last visit, I recalled how my apartment was in total disarray and was full of mildew. Just as the doctors had lost hope of me surviving my last accident, I had very little hope that my manuscript had survived weeks of being submerged underwater.

In March, 2006, I relocated back to the New Orleans area. Out of sheer curiosity, fueled by optimism and armed with hope, I went back to my old apartment and searched for the lost manuscript. After much searching, I found it. I was elated. But it was in very poor condition. All of the pages were faded and most were mildewed. I could not use it in that state. I would have to gently separate each page and rewrite each page, one by one. I was working three jobs. Where would I find the time to do this? But the Lord works in mysterious ways. I landed a job that allowed me to work as much overtime as I could handle. So I quit the three jobs I had and I worked only my one new job.

At first, I was assigned to work different posts. Then one day I was assigned to work a post that allowed me space to read and write. I retrieved my manuscript, from the trunk of my car, and I began the tedious task of rewriting it. Once I finished rewriting and re-reading it, I realized how vital the material in it was in today's society. Throughout the days and weeks, talk shows were discussing topics that I discussed in my book. I took that as a sign, and as confirmation. Suddenly, I felt that my book survived Katrina because it had something that many of my fellow Americans needed. And even though it was my third manuscript, I knew I had to offer this one first. Therefore, I determined that I would complete what I had started years before Katrina ever came. In the words of Jesus, "It is finished!"

I hope that this book will encourage and enlighten every soul that reads it. Thank you for your support. I elicit your prayers as I embark on my journey as a writer and author. Always remember: storms are as much a part of life as rain, wind, and sunshine. Don't allow any storm to cause you to lose your faith in God and what He has promised you. Your faith in God will get you through any storm. There is peace in the midst of a storm.

———◇※◇———

INTRODUCTION

I was born and raised in Amite, Louisiana. I am a product of what many may call a dysfunctional family. My mother met my father when she was a teenager. She married him at age seventeen. My father then joined the military. I was one of five children – four boys and one girl. My sister died shortly after birth. Years later, my infant brother died, leaving three boys. My mother had originally planned to name the first-born son after my father. Before she went into labor with her first child, she had an argument with my father. She ended up naming the child Jeremiah. I believe she did so out of spite. My sister was born next. I was the third child. By that time, my mother had forgiven my father, and consequently, I was named after him; James Jr. Seeing that I look just like him, I believe being named after my father was fate.

Upon my father's discharge from the military, he became a truck driver. It was a very lucrative profession for him. But my father loved to gamble. He loved playing cards and playing bingo. Gambling wasn't his only flaw. He was verbally and physically abusive to my mother. One day she grew tired of his abusive behavior and asked him to leave. I guess she felt that she could do bad all by herself. She didn't need a man to help her in that department. Years later, they divorced.

Although my father was under a court order to pay child support, he seldom paid. In fact, he chose to go to jail rather than pay my mom child support. I can recall one Christmas Eve, my father called from jail and pleaded with my mother to drop the charges against him so that he could get out. I started crying and pleading with my mother to get him out. In spite of all his faults, I loved my dad. In the Christmas spirit, she took pity on him and dropped the charges. Even though she knew in her heart that he wouldn't change, she showed him mercy.

My father was unaffected by his stay in jail. When he was released, he still refused to pay child support. You can lead a jackass to water but you can't make him drink. The fact that my father didn't pay child support didn't stop my mother from keeping food on the table, the lights on, clothes on our backs, and a roof over our heads. She worked two jobs to accomplish those tasks. My mother was determined to provide for her boys. Even though she was a good mother and provider, there were many nights I cried myself to sleep, longing for my dad.

When I was sixteen, I got the opportunity to go live with my dad. To put it mildly, I was ecstatic. To prevent redundancy, I will fast-forward past this chapter in my life. You can read about my adventure with my dad in the essay entitled, *Forgiveness: God's Prescription for Healing.*

After I graduated from high school and later completed one and a half years of college, I became a volunteer counselor at a correctional institution for juveniles. I worked alongside the institution's chaplain. Because of policy, I was restricted to the male offenders only. Male volunteers could have no interaction with the female inmates. In my role, I was responsible for conducting group bible studies and one-on-one counseling and rap sessions.

In the beginning, the group bible study was small. However, the inmates told their fellow inmates what a great time they had in the bible study and as a result, the attendance quickly escalated. Week after week, the bible study had more and more participants. I was so delighted with the participation and the attitudes in the sessions that I started bringing treats. I passed the treats around at the end of each weekly session. The boys were thrilled and excited about them.

The treats were an assortment of cookies, candies, pies, and chips. I know that some of the boys came just for the treats. But whatever the case may have been, I enjoyed each participant regardless of his reason for being there. Besides, the treats were rewards for participation in the bible study. And every participant contributed to the discussion.

The group bible study sessions were amazing, but I enjoyed the one-on-one sessions even more. During those sessions, the inmates would let down their walls, drop their defenses, and open up to me. In so doing, they would get personal with me and invite me to take a peek into their lives. They felt very comfortable with me and they didn't seem to mind pouring out their hearts. They said they could see my sincerity. They knew that I wasn't a paid employee of the state. Thus they felt that the only reason for my being there was because I genuinely cared about their well being. They were fully aware that the state of Louisiana didn't pay for any of the treats they enjoyed after the weekly sessions. They knew that blessing was coming from my pocket. Even though I was in my late twenties, at the time, and all of them were teenagers, they considered me a peer. Mind you, I was five-foot-three and I weighed 124 pounds. So I looked about as young as they were. I suppose that to them, I was a peer.

As I got to know these teenage inmates, I was stunned by what I learned about them. Nearly all of the boys I counseled believed that if their fathers had taken a more active role in their lives or had been a more positive role model for them, they would have turned out better and they wouldn't be in the predicament they were in. Many of them had fathers that were incarcerated or had been incarcerated. The vast majority of them said that their fathers smoked cigarettes, drank beer or alcohol, and either sold or used drugs. I believe that if a boy has either a positive father or a positive big brother - spiritual or biological - who takes an active role in his life, the odds of that boy becoming delinquent are greatly lowered. Here is a case in point: Notorious south central Los Angeles gang leader, Stanley Tookie Williams, wrote this in his memoir, *Blue Rage, Black Redemption*:

> *"As a youth I often felt emptiness in my life, and not simply for lack of a father's presence. My biological father was a sad example of fatherhood. I yearned for an esteemed black male figure who projected a dynamic image I could strive to emulate or surpass. In different circumstances my chances for success would have increased considerably."*

> *Dr. Martin Luther King, Jr. once said, "I can never be what I ought to be until you are what you ought to be." We (your sons) need you (our fathers) to be the best that you can be so that we can be the best that we can be. Boys learn more through the medium we call "observation." Boys are great imitators/*

emulators. If the truth be told, life is so much easier when you can follow a good example – a role model."

My father died on his birthday, which was January 14, 2000. Four weeks before his death, I visited him in the hospital. He was in a coma. I rubbed his forehead, sang him a gospel hymn, and told him that I had forgiven him. It was days after that visit (December 22, 1999), when I was struck by that speeding car while crossing Canal Street in downtown New Orleans. I attended my father's funeral on crutches.

Looking back to that hospital visit, it is clear that I hadn't truly forgiven him for not being a part of my life. My mouth said the words, but my heart didn't agree. Because I had cried so many times as a child, a teenager, and even as an adult, I refused to shed another tear on my father's behalf. In my heart, he had died many years ago. Two months later, I wrote a poem expressing how I felt about my father's passing. I titled it, *All Cried Out*. It is included in this book.

In October, 2000, I watched the movie *Jack Frost*. It's about a father who dies but gets a second chance to come back and make amends with his son. However, there's one problem: He comes back as a snowman and he has to find a way to convince his son that he, now a snowman, is his dad. It took him having to die for him to realize how special his son was and how much he had taken his son for granted.

Once the snowman convinced his son that he was his dad, the two bonded as father and son. At the end of the movie, I started to cry. I went into my mother's bathroom and wept like a kid. I cried and told God that I felt cheated. Life had cheated me out of the opportunity of experiencing the genuine love of a father. I also felt that my father had forfeited his rights to experience the love of a devoted son. I guess I wasn't *All Cried Out* after all.

A few days later, as I was reflecting on my father's lack of participation in my life, I received the inspiration for this book. It came in seasons. During the first season, I wrote epistles. It was amazing to me how these letters just flowed from within. It was as though I was an instrument in the hands of a gifted musician.

Each letter flowed from my soul like a sweet melody. I became a medium for someone to tell their story – sing their song – through me.

My mind was renewed with the birth of each letter. My soul was being restored. I envisioned fathers writing to their sons and sons writing to their fathers, expressing their innermost thoughts and emotions. My wounds began healing.

In the next season, rays of poetry illuminated my soul. These poems were about fathers and sons expressing their thoughts and feelings. Inspiration for this book came in fragments throughout the years. But there were periods of drought when no manna or rain fell from heaven. After I recovered this manuscript from my apartment in the wake of Katrina, the heavens opened and began to rain down on my soul in the form of essays. I wrote as I was moved and inspired.

As I penned each essay, I realized that stories could be told from multiple angles and from different sides. Because all men are not alike or on the same page in life, I realized that one essay may appeal or minister to one man, but not to another. It is my hope that men will see themselves in one of the different essays, and those that need to will then make the choice to be a real man.

I was pleased with the letters, poems, and essays, but I felt something was missing. In March, 2007, the final season blossomed. As I was visiting my former church, God had me to focus on the pastor, Rev. Daniel Muse, Sr. As he was expounding on the Word of God, I was led to include him in my book. But how?

At the conclusion of the service and as I was driving back to New Orleans, I had an epiphany. It became clear to me how I was going to add Pastor Muse to my book. I would interview him, his wife, and children. This book is composed of four sections which I call seasons: Essays (Spring), Poems (Summer), Letters (Fall), and Interviews (Winter). I believe the full effect of this book will be felt by reading all four seasons, then allowing the seasons to minister to your mind, body, and soul.

I have seen many young boys, young men, and even grown men shed tears due to their unhealed wounds caused by an estranged father. It is my prayer that something contained in this book will touch the lives of many fathers and draw them closer to their sons. This book is a blend of fiction and nonfiction. I endeavor to enlighten fathers on how important they are to their sons. I am sharing intimate details of my life in hopes of accomplishing this mission. How priceless it would be to hear a man say about his son what God said about Jesus: "This is my beloved Son, in whom I am well pleased." (Matthew 3:17) Allow me to paraphrase that: *This is my son whom I love dearly. Not only do I love him, I am also very proud of him!* Show me one young man who wouldn't be deeply moved by such an affirmation.

Here's one final thought: Too many woman are burdened with the awesome task of trying to transform boys into men. A woman can teach a boy many valuable life lessons; however, a woman can never teach a boy how to be a man. Fathers, that's your responsibility. Don't shun or run away from this responsibility. Don't pass the buck to another man. Be responsible. Step up to the plate and hit a homerun in the lives of your sons. It may be a Grand Slam. They don't ask for much. Just time and attention. They are priceless jewels, longed for from deep inside their hearts, and treasured for all eternity.

A SPECIAL MESSAGE
FOR MOTHERS

I cannot end this book without sowing into the lives of mothers – the bedrock of our families. Because this message is so dear to my heart, I had to place it after the Introduction. Although this book is intended to minister to fathers and sons, I realize the fact that many women, especially mothers, will read it as well. Therefore, I want to deposit some words of wisdom into their spirit.

The Bible declares: "Man is the image and glory of God: but the woman is the glory of the man" (1 Corinthians 11:7). When Adam, the first man, was created, the Lord God said, "It is not good that the man should be alone" (Genesis 2:18). Therefore, He made man a companion – woman. God caused a deep sleep to come upon Adam. While he slept, God took one of his ribs and made woman. The first woman came out of man; henceforth, every man now comes out of woman in the form of a baby boy.

It's been said that behind every good man stands a good woman. I understand the theory of that statement; however, it devalues the essence of a real woman. Personally, I believe that beside, not behind, every good man stands a great woman. This repositioning makes woman one with man. Woman plays a pivotal role in man reaching the pinnacle of his potential. Martin Luther King said, in his autobiography: "If I have done anything in this struggle, it is because I have had behind me and at my side a devoted, understanding, dedicated, patient companion in the person of my wife."

I highly respect Dr. King for honoring his wife, Coretta – the woman at his side, supporting him to the fullest. Many men have the misconception that just because a woman is beautiful, sexy, and feminine, she is also weak and fragile. This is far from the truth. A real woman doesn't have a problem investing her time, talents, energy, and finances in what's hers – her man, her family, her home. In a heartbeat, she will roll up her sleeves and do whatever is necessary to support and provide for her family. She can be strong, soft and delicate, simultaneously.

In fact, that is the real reason God brought her forth – out of man. Within her, she possesses the power to be one of man's greatest assets, or she can be his worst liability. She can be a source of strength unto him or a weak link that can bring about his downfall. Ask Samson. He can bear witness to this fact. Let's explore further why God made woman.

After God created Adam, He put him in the Garden of Eden to dress it and keep it – to work it (Genesis 2:15). God then brought all the beasts of the field and the fowl of the air unto Adam to name. Once Adam gave all God's creatures names, God saw that all the creatures had mates, except Adam. He realized that man would get lonely and would be in need of someone on his level to confide in and draw comfort and strength from, as well as someone to work alongside him and help him dress and keep the garden.

Although everything God created was good, nothing was qualified or capable enough to be a helpmeet to Adam – man. With this in mind, God caused a deep sleep to come upon Adam. It is my belief that the reason God put Adam to sleep is because He needed one of Adam's ribs, not his advice or opinion. God made Adam a helpmeet, a companion – Eve, the first woman.

When Adam woke up from his deep sleep, God presented Eve to him. Adam declared, "This is now bone of my bones and flesh of my flesh" (Genesis 2:23). In other words, Adam declared that he and Eve were one – one mind, one body, one soul. When they consummated their relationship, Eve conceived and had a son. She said, "I have acquired a man from the Lord" (Genesis 4:1).

God exalted woman to motherhood – the greatest position she will ever occupy in life. I don't care if a woman is CEO of one of the world's largest corporations, President of the United States, crowned Miss America, or grows up to be Oprah Winfrey, she will NEVER occupy a more exalted position than that of motherhood. Children's Defense Fund Founder, Marian Wright Edelman, once said: "If you are a parent, recognize that this is the most important calling and rewarding challenge you have. What you do every day, what you say and how you act, will do more to shape the future of America than any other factor."

For the purpose of this book, I want this message to concentrate on a mother's role in the life of her son. As a mother, you have a unique bond with your son. This bond begins in the embryonic stage and extends far beyond the cutting of the umbilical cord. From conception to delivery, your son grows inside your womb – feeding off your strengths, and your weaknesses, and receiving nourishment from your body. Being the emotional creature that you are, next to God, you are your son's greatest source of comfort. Let's use fictional little Jimmy as an example.

Jimmy is four years old. He falls and hurts himself and starts to cry. His father yells, "Stop crying like a little girl! You're a soldier. Take it like a man. Do you want me to give you something to cry for?"

Quickly, you come to Jimmy's defense saying, "Leave him alone! Can't you see he's hurt? Let mommy kiss that baby's bobo." You would then hold Jimmy in your arms, pat him on his back, and tell him everything is going to be alright. In the twinkling of an eye, Jimmy would be smiling again. His father would then say, "You're going to make that boy a li'l sissy." Once again, you would come to Jimmy's defense and say, "Don't worry about your daddy. You are mommy's li'l man."

To be perfectly honest, I believe most men are little boys at heart. When we get sick, we want that same treatment little Jimmy received when he fell and hurt himself. We want to be caressed, comforted, and assured that everything is going to be alright. Instead of that pat on the back, we want our forehead rubbed and stroked. That's the main reason many of us go home to our mother when we get sick. Moms seem to have that special angelic touch.

That special bond that exists between mother and son should never be taken for granted. A mother's love is priceless. Regardless of the issues you have with his father, you should never handicap your son with your words. Jesus said, "The words that I speak unto you, they are spirit and they are life" (John 6:63). The tongue is a powerful instrument. It can heal or it can wound. It can spread joy or it can inflict pain. It can uplift or it can tear down. It can bless or it can curse. "Death and life are in the power of the tongue" (Proverbs 18:21).

As a child, I was made to believe this fallacy: "Sticks and stones may break my bones, but words can never hurt me." That is a lie from the pits of hell. Words can indeed cause great pain. They leave deep scars and lasting wounds. You must be very mindful of the words you speak into the ears of your son or sons. In the beginning, life did not exist until God said, "Let there be …" Until He spoke the Word.

Words have the potential to become self-fulfilling prophecies. When you say to your son, "You are stupid just like your 'good-for-nothing' dad!" those words may ring true one day. Don't allow your frustrations with your son's father to overshadow your responsibility to properly raise your son. Please don't let bitterness cloud your good judgment. Help your son become a better man by speaking positive words into his spirit. Never forget that a boy is a man in training.

Although you can't teach your son how to be a man, you can instill within him some ethics, values, and principles that will build his character and which can ultimately make him a better man. By speaking uplifting words into your son's life and being a positive influence on him, you pave a smoother road for the woman who may someday become your daughter-in-law. It is your responsibility to sow the right seeds into his life in order to reap a better harvest.

Let your son see the essence of a real woman in you – his mother. It's been said that most men are attracted to women who remind them of their mother. The better role model you set for your son, the better the chances of him later selecting a good mate or companion. Bear this in mind: his respect or lack of respect for women will stem from his relationship with you – his mother.

As part of the unique bond shared between mother and son, boys are generally very protective of their mothers, especially their single or divorced mothers. I know when I was a teenager, I was. In my mom's glory days, the 70s and 80s, she was what we called, a *fox*! She had it going on, and she knew it. She was a *brick house*. I don't mean any disrespect, but my mom was a hot *li'l shorty* with plenty of *back*. My mom is a four-feet, eleven-inch tall redbone. They used to call her *Li'l Bit*. Back in the day, she enjoyed wearing tight-fitting clothing, which included a pair of black leather pants.

There were many times when I walked behind her so that the men in the neighborhood couldn't check out her backside. Today, the young folks call that *blocking*. It was one thing to have the men in my community trying to push up on my mom. But I also had to contend with the remarks of my mannish classmates. For example, one day my mom came to my school, Amite High. I don't remember the reason for her visit. She was wearing something tight-fitting. When she arrived on campus, some of my classmates said, "That's your mom? Boy, I'm going to be your step-dad." I now realize that it was only their hormones talking. Not one of them was ready to handle the responsibility of working, paying bills, and caring for a woman with three teenage boys. Truth be told, my father couldn't even handle that responsibility, and he claimed to be a man. That's why boys should stick with girls. There is a tremendous difference between a woman and a girl. A big difference.

Someone once asked the question, "Can you pay my bills?" That is the sentiment of many women. This world has many women who are looking for a sugar daddy – a man to pay their bills. Man was not created to help a woman pay her bills. On the contrary, woman was created to be man's helpmeet – his soul mate. Together, they are one mind, one body, and one soul. When man and woman work together in harmony, they complement one another. You see, a real man is nobody's sugar daddy. He is a provider. Providing for his family is a chief component of his character. A real man will bring home a loaf of bread, not a slice of bread. You can't feed a family off a slice of bread but you can work wonders with a loaf.

Being a good provider encompasses more than just paying bills. A lot more. Many women have made some poor choices in the men they have selected to share their beds with. As a result, they are forever connected to that individual because of the child they created. You may have many issues with your son's father; however, your issues are not your son's issues. Allow your son, through his relationship or lack of relationship with his father, to develop his own set of issues. I am very grateful that my mother allowed me the opportunity to reach my own conclusions about my dad based on my own personal experiences with him. That means a lot to me. I may have reached the same conclusions as her; however, at least she didn't contaminate my judgment.

Also, never use your son as a weapon or pawn to try to manipulate his dad. Just because you feel your rights were violated, that doesn't give you just cause to violate your son's rights by denying him the chance to have a relationship with his father. Your son's father may not have been a very good boyfriend or husband; however, don't deny him the opportunity to be a good father to his son. He may surprise you by being an excellent father. There is a chance your son may have a better relationship with his father than you had. He deserves the opportunity to connect with his dad. If your son plans to lead a balanced life, he needs the support of both his parents, whether or not the two of them are a couple. As his mother, you should always make your son's welfare your top priority. Regardless of the fact that his father may or may not exemplify the qualities of a real man, he is still your son's father. Your son didn't choose his dad. You did. Therefore, don't give your son's father the power to turn you, a real woman, into anything short of being just that – a real woman. Your son needs to see a real woman in action. You must be that example. Keep in mind that you may be the standard by which your son uses to compare all other women.

I feel compelled to mention this incident. One day I got into a heated dispute with one of my co-workers. I was telling him, and a young lady, about my book that I was in the process of self-publishing. I told them my motivation for writing the book. I said that a lot of men have neglected their responsibilities to their children, especially to their sons. As a result, many boys have grown up to be hard. Thus, they lack a true concept or understanding of what it means to be a real man. Many men have travelled down the road of being deadbeat dads.

When I made that remark, the young lady said, "I am a father and a mother to my two sons." I looked at her and said, "A woman can never be a father to a child and neither can a father be a mother to a child." I opened a can of worms when I said that. The young man was quick to offer his input. He said, "The bible says, 'God will be a mother to the motherless.'" I informed him that the bible never said that. I told him that a preacher must have felt inspired to say that in his message one day and he probably got a lot of *Amens* from the congregation. As a result, the phrase quickly spread like a wildfire. Subsequently, preachers across the nation used it in their sermons. I told him that nowhere in the bible is God referred to as a mother. We are always instructed to entreat God as Our Father.

Feeling very sure of himself, he said, "I can do all things through Christ." I looked at him and said, "I would like to see you get pregnant and have a baby. The only way a man can ever be a mother to a child is if he can get pregnant and carry that child to term in his womb, feeling it kicking and growing inside of him. A man doesn't have the proper equipment to be a mother to a child. He can never breastfeed a baby. The same goes for a woman. She can never replace a father. Without the ministry of a man, a woman can never become a mother. And without the ministry of a woman, a man can never become a father. The best a woman can be to a child is a helluva mother." He was speechless. He walked away like a dog with his tail tucked between his legs. I wasn't trying to have a piss match with him. I was just proving my point.

Noted author and social activist, Sister Souljah, wrote in her memoir, *No Disrespect*: "If a son is raised with no father, he will lack the criteria for understanding what it is to be a man. Instead, he may look toward the guys in the street. Moreover, if a young boy has a father that takes no responsibility for his wife and family, then he will grow up to believe that he need not take such responsibility either." Fathers and mothers are parents. Parents are caregivers. Nurturing and providing for their child is the core of their very existence. Some parents take this to heart, while others take it for granted. It is a parent's responsibility to provide for his or her child. A good mother can provide for her child with or without the input of the child's father if she has to. Countless mothers have done fantastic jobs raising their children without help from the child's father. It's not an easy task; however, many mothers have answered the call and risen to the occasion. I applaud those mothers and I give them a standing ovation.

As I conclude this special message, I want to share my personal testimony with you. Although I look like my father, I am nothing like him. I take after my mother. My mother is a very spiritual woman. She is a woman of prayer. Regardless of how bleak or dismal our circumstances or situations may have appeared, my mother never lost faith in the power of prayer. She holds fast to her belief that if you pray, God will make a way. When my brothers and I were young, I can't recall a night that she didn't have us kneel beside our bed and recite "The Lord's Prayer" or the "Now I Lay Me Down To Sleep" prayer before we got in bed and drifted off to sleep. We rented a two-bedroom house. My brothers and I slept in the same bed – two at the head and the other in the middle at the foot. It's amazing that I have a plethora of my mother's attributes.

The list is numerous, but I would like to draw your attention to one quality I am most proud to have gleaned from my mom. Even though she is a small woman, she is a very hard worker. She knows how to plant herself like a tree on the banks of a river and maintain a job for a long period of time. Unlike many people, she isn't tossed to and fro like a leaf in the wind, drifting from job to job. She believes in giving a day's work for a day's pay. I share that same philosophy. I believe that a job is a workplace and not a social hall. I go to work to work, not to socialize. If I make a friend at work, I count it a blessing. I know of a lot of young men who can't seem to keep a job. It's sad that many of them can stay in jail longer than they can stay on a job. Thanks to the example set by my mother, I have never had that problem.

My mom taught me the value of hard work and self-reliance. Because of her training, I can cook, clean, do laundry, and hold down a job. Although I don't sew, I know how to sew. Even though she didn't teach me how to be a man, her input into my life has helped me to become a better man. She is one of my role models. It is my dream to become successful enough so that I can give her everything my father couldn't and wouldn't give her. She is worthy of that and so much more. So mothers, if you raise your sons properly and instill strong work ethics in them, they may do the same for you one day. "Faith is the substance of things hoped for, the evidence of things not seen" (Hebrews 11:1). Trust and have faith in God. Unlike any human, He won't disappoint you.

WINTER
INTERVIEWS

BIOGRAPHY OF REVEREND DANIEL MUSE, SR.

On Sunday, March 4, 2007, I sat in on the worship service at Greater Community Church of God in Christ in Amite, Louisiana, where Reverend Daniel Muse, Sr. is the pastor. As I scanned the congregation and focused my attention on the pulpit, I observed two seats to the right of the podium where the pastor and his wife were sitting, like a king with his queen at his right side. As I turned my attention to the choir stand and the section that was designated for the musicians, I noticed the pastor's sons. His oldest son, Antonyo (Tony), is a minister, the church organist and the choir director. His other son, Victor, is a deacon and the drummer for the church. Coming out of the office is his daughter, Margaret, who is the office manager for the church, a member of the choir, and a committee president. Junior, their youngest son, played bass guitar with the church musicians. He died of congestive heart failure a few years ago. As long as I can remember, Pastor Muse's family has been at his side, supporting his vision. At that moment, I knew that the Muse family was the reason why the Lord had directed me to sit in on the service. God wanted me to include the Muse family in my book. Standing in front of me, proclaiming God's Word, was the epitome of a real man.

Daniel is the son of Brother Peter Muse, Sr. and Sister Carlee Foster Muse. He was the twelfth of their sixteen children. His infant brother, David, died shortly after birth, as did a set of twin girls. That left five boys and eight girls. Daniel's father was a farmer and a local evangelist. His mother was a homemaker and a church mother. His parents, especially his mother, taught him how to face and handle spiritual opposition when it arises. They told him that if he would hold his peace and not fight back or retaliate, the Lord would fight all his battles (1 Samuel 17:45-47). They taught him humility and patience. His mother would often tell him, "If your cause is right and just, just stand. Truth and justice will always come out on top in the end." Daniel kept those words close to his heart. They became his shield.

At age fifteen, Daniel accepted the Lord and got saved. In March of 1956, at a revival meeting at Amite # 1 Church of God in Christ, Daniel received the Baptism of the Holy Ghost in what was known as a Tarry Service. That same night, the Lord called him to preach and he accepted that calling. Daniel had faced opposition his whole life. As a young preacher, he was often told that he would never amount to anything. Back in the day, the Church of God in Christ was called the Sanctified Church. It was known for its hell-fire-and-brimstone style of preaching. The youth of the church were continuously told, "It is better to marry than to burn." As a young minister, Daniel took that to heart; therefore, at the age of nineteen, he married his seventeen-year-old girlfriend.

The young couple later had a son. They named him Ronald. The burden and responsibility of being the wife of a preacher was overwhelming and became too much for the young bride to bear. After only three years of marriage, Daniel and his young bride ended their marriage. However, they remained friends until her death.

One Sunday evening at the church, a young girl named Bobbie, visiting with her sister, caught Daniel's eye. Bobbie continued to visit. A friendship began to blossom between them. About five months later, Bobbie made a call to Daniel on his job. They became a couple after that. Two years later, in April, 1966, Daniel and Bobbie were married. For Daniel however, opposition in his life rose again, like a seven-headed dragon. Many people opposed Daniel's and Bobbie's marriage because of Daniel's previous marriage.

But they decided to obey God rather than man. To be fruitful and multiply. He and Bobbie were blessed with four children – Antonyo (Tony), Margaret, Victor, and Daniel Jr. (Junior). Some time later, Daniel and

Bobbie honored Bobbie's Aunt Hazel's dying request. They took in her foster daughter, Cicely, to raise her as part of their family. Cicely would prove to be a wonderful addition to the Muse family.

Daniel is faithful to his spiritual and natural family. Because of his faithfulness, God promoted him to the office of Pastor and gave him a vision for a church. *Where there is no vision, the people perish* (Proverbs 29:18). God told Daniel to name his church "Community Church of God in Christ." Community Church would be a beacon of hope for the community, a sanctuary for weary souls, and a temple of worship for born-again believers.

On July 28, 1974, Community Church opened its doors and held its first worship service. That dragon known as opposition once again spewed fire. Daniel was told that the church would flop and he would fall flat on his face. Daniel's opposition didn't come from those who where outside the church. All of his opposition, like crabs in a bucket, came from church leaders and so-called saints – people inside the church community. The bible teaches that a prophet is a true prophet if what he says comes to pass. I guess they were lying prophets because Community Church (now called Greater Community) has been standing for the past thirty-three years and is growing stronger and more vibrant with each passing day. It is one of the most successful churches in its area.

God has richly blessed Reverend Muse's ministry. He is the State Evangelist in the Third Ecclesiastical Jurisdiction of Eastern Louisiana of the Churches of God in Christ and the District Superintendent of District Nine. Reverend Muse seems to have the Midas Touch. Everything he touches seems to prosper. He and Bobbie have been married for forty-one years and he has been the pastor of Greater Community for thirty-three years.

In June, 2003, the very foundation of Reverend Muse's faith was shaken when his youngest son, Daniel Jr. (Junior), died of congestive heart failure. Junior had been diagnosed with heart disease a few years prior to his death. He had always complained of shortness of breath. Losing a son that bears your name is a blow that can shake the foundation of even the strongest father. That blow knocked the wind out of Reverend Muse. But while he was rising to his feet, recovering from that, Reverend Muse received a second blow. Doctors diagnosed his other son, Victor, with the same condition that claimed the life of Junior. But like the Prophet Daniel in the

Old Testament, Reverend Muse has always been a man of prayer. That's why his church and family are both successful. Reverend Muse stays on his knees, always in prayer, entreating the face of God and seeking God's will for his life, family, and ministry. If God be for you, who can be against you?

INTERVIEW WITH REVEREND DANIEL MUSE, SR.

Today is Saturday, March 10, 2007. It is nine forty-five in the morning. I have decided to run inside Wal-Mart to pick up a pack of back-up cassette tapes for my interviews with the Muse family. My first interview is with Reverend Muse at ten o'clock this morning. I can't stand being late or unprepared. I drive up at Reverend Muse's home at exactly ten o'clock. Reverend Muse had just walked outside. Seeing me, he greets me and comments on my punctuality. Although I arrived at exactly ten o'clock, I am late by my personal standards. He invites me inside and we each take a seat at the kitchen table. His wife is in the back, organizing her day. I set up my tape recorder and begin recording. "A Real Man Stands Tall, an interview with Rev. Daniel Muse, Sr. Good morning, sir."

"Good morning," he replied.

"Let's begin."

Author: **What was your relationship like with your father?**

Daniel: My father and I had a real good relationship. He was a farmer. I was the baby boy. When I became a teenager, I was the only boy left at home; therefore, I spent a lot of time with my father. My father was an evangelist. Since I was the only one at home with a driver's license, I drove my father around a lot.

This gave us even more time to bond. My father had a heart for sick folks. I often drove him around to visit and pray for the sick. He loved sharing God's Word. It didn't matter if you were black or white, my father would talk bible with you. As I said, he loved sharing God's Word.

Author: **What do you remember most about your father?**

Daniel: My father was born in 1872. He had no formal education. Although he was an uneducated man, he was well educated in the scriptures – God's Word. My father knew scripture like the back of his hands. I got my love and appreciation for scripture from my father. He was a hard-working, honest man. I learned how to rear a family and interact with my boys from my father.

Author: **What was the greatest life lesson your father taught you?**

Daniel: My father taught me to be honest, to be fair, to trust God, to trust His Word, and to stand on His Word. He told me that I would have great success if I did these things.

Author: **What did you learn about being a husband from the way your father treated your mother?**

Daniel: My father had great affection and much respect for my mother. He always addressed her as Sister Carlee, and she referred to him as Brother Peter. They worked together as a team. My parents were never separated. No matter how rough times may have been, they always managed to hold things together.

Author: **What was your relationship like with your mother?**

Daniel: My mother and I were real tight. We were real tight. She taught me how to be faithful, how to be committed. She was the type of saint who went to church, faithfully, every Tuesday night, Friday night, Sunday morning, and Sunday night. Remember, I was the only child left at home with a driver's license; therefore, I was always in church with her because I had to drive. She taught me how to keep a house clean. My mother believed that the upkeep of the house was everyone's responsibility. She was the type of person who couldn't stand a dirty house or yard. She taught us that cleanliness is next to godliness. You may not believe this, but my mother taught me how to hustle. She believed that every man and woman should know how to hustle. When school was out, I would go with her to pick strawberries or snap beans. My father was a farmer; therefore, she didn't have to have a side hustle. But anytime extra work came available, she would take us along with her. She taught me the value of a dollar and how to manage money. My mother always had money. She always held back a piece of money for a rainy day.

My mother was a homemaker. She loved to can preserves – peaches, pears, blackberries, and whatnot. She enjoyed making quilts. She taught us all how to patch our clothes. That's right. My mother taught me how to sew. My wife doesn't know how good I can really sew. My mother loved for us to go to school with freshly pressed and starched clothes. To this day, I can't stand dirty clothes.

Author: **Did your relationship with your mother prepare you for your relationship with your wife?**

Daniel: Yes. My mother never overruled my father. She worked with him and they were always of one accord. Whenever we wanted to go somewhere or do something, we would always ask mama first. She would always tell us to go ask our daddy. When we would ask our father, he would say, "What did your mama say?" What that taught me was to always be in agreement with my wife. I learned that marriage isn't a dictatorship. It's a partnership.

Author: **How did your father treat your mother?**

Daniel: My father treated my mother with much honor and respect. He gave her free rein. He fully trusted her judgment. For example: Three of my sisters lived in New Orleans. There were many times my mother would feel led to go see about her girls. It did not matter what time of day or night it was. It could be 12 o'clock midnight. If my mother felt led to go check on her daughters, she would tell my father, and we would strike out to go visit my sisters. Sometimes we would be gone as long as a week before we returned home. My father would never question my mother because he trusted her. Now when my mother would be on the go too much, my father would let her know and she would be submissive. From watching how they interacted with each other, I learned how a good marriage should be run. I also learned that trust is an essential factor in a marriage. My parents had a wonderful marriage because they loved and trusted one another.

Author: **What advice did your father give you on marriage and family?**

Daniel: Whenever I had a question about marriage, my father would direct my attention to the scriptures. He told me to read Ephesians chapter five. In Ephesians you will find these words: "So men ought to love their wives as their own bodies. He that loveth his wife loveth himself. For no man ever hated his own flesh; but nourisheth and cherisheth it even as the Lord does the church. For we are members of his body, of his flesh, and of his bones. For this cause shall a man leave his father and mother, and shall be joined unto his wife, and the two shall become one flesh. This is a great mystery: but I speak concerning Christ and the church. Nevertheless, let every one of you in particular so love his wife, even as himself, and the wife see that she reverence her husband" (Ephesians 5:28-33). My father taught me that long before I got married. He taught me the responsibility of the man of the house. He taught me how to provide for my family. My father was a great provider. I never had a hungry day in my life when I lived under my father's roof. He was a great farmer. Whatever he raised on the farm graced our table. We had meat and vegetables in abundance. Not just our family, my father always gave food to other families within our community who were in need.

Author: **What is a father's role in the family?**

Daniel: A father's role in the family is to be the head of his family. He must set the tempo – take the lead role. He sets the pace. He is the example. My father was the first one to get up in the morning. He would walk through the house and make sure that the house was in order – secure. On Sundays, he made sure that the entire household was in church.

Author: **How does your relationship with God influence you as a man, husband, and father?**

Daniel: My relationship with God keeps me grounded. It keeps me out of trouble. It keeps me faithful and committed to my marriage and my family. My relationship with God is the very foundation for my manhood and my family. God has allowed me to travel all across America to preach the Gospel – the message of *Good News*. I have to be an example of what I preach. In other words, I have to put into practice what I preach. My entire life has been involved in ministry. It's all I know. My family is a vital part of my ministry.

Author: **What is a mother's role in the family?**

Daniel: A mother's role in the family is to make a house a home. Just like a father, a mother has to provide for her family. Like the Holy Spirit, a mother is a comforter. She provides love, care, and comfort for the whole family, including her husband. In the book of Proverbs it says: *A wise woman builds her house but a foolish woman plucks it down with her hands.* She compliments her husband – makes him look good before the world. She makes sure that her children are well-mannered and well-trained. It's a mother's responsibility to teach the boys and girls how to be homemakers, how to adjust, how to play the hand life deals them.

Author: **Did I hear you correctly? Did you say that boys and girls should learn how to be homemakers?**

Daniel: Yes. All my boys can cook and clean house. My sons can survive all by themselves if they have to. All my sons are married with kids. If their wives should go on strike and refuse to cook, clean up, or do laundry, all is well. All my boys know how to cook, how to clean, how to wash and fold clothes, and how to iron. My wife and I raised our children to be independent and self-sufficient.

Missionary Muse enters the kitchen and takes a seat at the kitchen table and sits on my left, directly across from her husband, and catches the tail end of her husband's interview.

Author: **What is your relationship like with your sons?**

Daniel: I have a great relationship with my boys. My youngest son, Junior, died at the age of twenty-seven. My oldest son, Antonyo – we call him Tony. My second son's name is Victor. This past week, me, Tony, and Victor were down at the church's pond. We are having some landscaping work done on a piece of property that is owned by the church. We were down there overseeing the work – talking, laughing, teasing one another. We set up a plastic bottle to use for target practice. We each took turns shooting at the bottle. To no avail, not one of us could hit the target. We laughed and teased each other on our poor marksmanship. My sons and I constantly get together and talk. They always ask me for my advice. We have such a great relationship that I often ask for their advice. Just because I am their father, that doesn't mean that I know everything and have all the answers. They may see something that I failed to see or they may see it in another light – provide a different angle, perspective.

Author: **How did the death of Daniel Jr. affect your faith?**

Daniel: Immediately after the doctor told me that my son had died, I went into a state of depression. Up until this season in my life, I never knew that a minister or saint could be depressed. The enemy was at war with me in my mind. He told me, *You have prayed for people on their deathbeds and God has healed them. You prayed for your son and God didn't heal him. Will you still pray for the sick and tell them that God is a healer? Do you still have faith in God?* As I pondered these things, the Spirit of the Lord spoke to my heart and encouraged my spirit. He put me in remembrance of Psalms 34:1, which reads, "I will bless the Lord at all times; his praises shall continually be in my mouth." In all things I count it all joy (from James, Chapter 1). The death of Junior was rough, but my faith in God is still intact.

Author: **If today was your last day of life, what do you want your sons to remember most about you?**

Daniel: I want them to know that I was a good father and that I did my best with the hand that life dealt me. I didn't give them everything they wanted, but I met all their needs. They were never hungry because I always worked. I want them to know that I treated their mother like she was a queen. I teach them to treat their wives the way I treat their mother. I want them to know that I was a good preacher and that I practiced everything I preached. Not only was I a good preacher, a good husband, a good father, I was also a good friend. I want them to know that they were my friends and that I love them. I have no regrets.

Author: **What one piece of advice would you like to give to young men today?**

Daniel: It is so simple. I don't see why men don't get it. It's handed to the fathers. They spend their whole lives seeking after material things – food, clothes, automobiles, houses, land, longevity. I base my whole life on the scriptures. I can thank my father for giving me my love for the scriptures – God's Word. In the sixth chapter of the book of Matthew, there is an order for men to live by. The entire chapter can be summed up in these three verses: "For after all these things do the Gentiles seek. For your heavenly Father knoweth that ye have need of all these things. But seek ye first the kingdom of God and His righteousness, and all these things shall be added unto you. Take therefore no thought for the morrow, for the morrow shall take thought for the things of itself. Sufficient unto the day is the evil thereof" (Matthew 6:32-34). If we put God first, all these things – education, money, cars, fine homes, food, good health, family, and long life – will be given unto us.

I concluded my interview with Rev. Muse and turned my attention to his lovely wife, Missionary Bobbie Muse.

INTERVIEW WITH
MISSIONARY BOBBIE MUSE

I have just ended my interview with Rev. Muse. Missionary Muse has recently joined us at the kitchen table in their home. I place the tape recorder down and begin recording. "A Real Man Stands Tall, an interview with Missionary Bobbie Muse. Good morning."

"Good morning," she replied.

Author: **How did you and Daniel meet?**

Bobbie: I was a young girl, and I wanted to get out of the house. I grew tired of staying home on Sunday nights. One Sunday night my sister and her boyfriend decided to visit Amite #1 Church of God in Christ, and I decided to tag along with them. Daniel was a youth minister there. Each time I visited his church, he was very kind and nice to me. We would talk and he would ask me various questions. About five months later, I called him on his job, and we officially started dating.

Author: **What attracted you to Daniel?**

Bobbie: I was attracted to Daniel's personality. Every time I visited his church, he was nice and cordial. I could see that he loved the Lord and I enjoyed his gentleness.

Author: **How long have you and Daniel been married?**

Bobbie: Daniel and I dated for two years before we got married. We have been married now for forty-one years.

Author: **What's Daniel like as a husband?**

Bobbie: He is a wonderful husband. He is humble and courteous. He is kind and affectionate. He is very respectful. He gives me the best of him, and I give him the best of me. He is my bedrock, my leaning post – the apple of my eye. Our marriage isn't perfect. We have our share of storms like every marriage; however, we don't let the sun go down on our anger. I am a blessed woman to have Daniel as my husband. I love him very much.

Author: **What's Daniel like as a father?**

Bobbie: He loves his children. He has always put their needs above his own. He believes in the scriptures: "Train up a child in the way he should go, and when he is old he will not depart from it" (Proverbs 22:6). He is a great disciplinarian and provider. He wants the best for them. Although we didn't always give them the best – name brands or what have you – we always gave them the best of us. Daniel expects the boys to be faithful to God, faithful to the community, faithful to their wives, and faithful to their families. He expects the girls to be committed to God, committed to their husbands, and committed to their families as well. Our marriage serves as a role model for theirs. He believes that a father should leave some type of inheritance for his children. His death shouldn't be a burden to his children.

Author: **What's the one quality you admire the most about Daniel?**

Bobbie: What I admire the most about Daniel is his spirit of excellence. He loves for things to be done in decency and in order. I love that he is dependable. I can count on him because I know, from his track record, he will be there.

Author: **The first-born son is usually named after his father. Why did you bestow this honor on your youngest son?**

Bobbie: That's a long story. Every family has a Junior. I did not want a Junior. I wanted each of my children to have their own identity. I wanted all my children's name to start with the letter *A*. My first child was a boy. I named him Antonyo. We call him Tony. My next child was a girl. I named her Margaret Antonette. My next child was another boy. I named him Victor. Somehow, I got off-track from my plan to keep all my children's names beginning with the letter A. *I thought to myself: maybe you named him after Victor Newman on The Young and the Restless.* After Victor, I had no plans for any more kids. Daniel looked at me and said, "I'm gon' keep sending you back until you give me a *Junior*." When I got pregnant the last time, I told Daniel, "If it's a boy, you can name him whatever you like." It was a boy, and he named him Daniel Jr.

Author: **How did the death of Daniel Jr. affect your marriage and family?**

Bobbie: The death of Junior left a void in my life, my marriage, and my heart. There was such emptiness inside of me that I could not explain. Daniel couldn't fill that void. So many days I would just cry and ask God, Why me? Junior was my baby. We were close. Although Daniel was hurting too, he couldn't feel my pain. I carried Junior for nine months. He grew inside my womb. I felt like I couldn't go on without him. At first I was angry. I am committed and faithful to God. Why my son? Junior wasn't a bad child. He had never been in trouble with the law. He had a kind heart. I know this may sound bad, but it is how I felt. I felt that God should have taken one of those thugs out there on the streets who have no respect for the law or others and left my baby. But then I realized that a mother would still be in pain. One day I realized that I had other children and a husband that needed me to go on. God wants the best. That's why he took Junior. God never makes mistakes. So why not me?

Author: **What's the most romantic thing Daniel has ever done for you?**

Bobbie: It was our anniversary. While I was at church, Daniel had some of the ladies from the church to come to our home and decorated our bedroom. We have a fireplace in our bedroom. They placed decorations and candles all around the bedroom and fireplace. When I made it home, they had romantic music playing and champagne glasses set up with sparkling flavored water. We had the house all to ourselves. I was deeply moved that he went through all that trouble for me. That's the type of husband he is.

Author: **Has Daniel ever cooked for you or helped with household chores?**

Bobbie: When the kids were younger, I used to work for National Grocery Store and Daniel worked for the school system. He would get off work at three o'clock and I would get off at six or sometimes later. He would pick the kids up from school, bring them home, and tend to them. While I was at work, he would cook and he and the kids would clean up the house. There were many evenings I came home to a clean house and a home-cooked meal. Now that Daniel is a lot older and the children are all grown up, he doesn't cook anymore. He loves to barbecue on the grill. Our oldest son, Tony, inherited that skill from his father. He operates a small restaurant within the city limits. People can't get enough of his barbecue ribs. On last night, Daniel and I were laying in bed. I mentioned to him that I had a taste for an egg sandwich. Daniel got up and left the room. I had no idea that he was in the kitchen preparing my request. When he returned to the bedroom, I feasted off of my egg sandwich. Daniel is a wonderful man, husband, and father.

Author: **What's your idea of a real man?**

Bobbie: A real man is a man who loves God, loves family, and loves his community. The reason I believe that a real man is a man who loves God is because it's God who makes a man a man.

I ended my interviews with Rev. Muse and his wife and thanked them for sharing their morning with me. I informed them of the premise of the book. Then I told them I believed that their interviews validated my book.

INTERVIEW WITH ANTONYO "TONY" MUSE, SR.

After I finished interviewing Missionary Muse, I phoned Tony and asked him for his location. He informed me that he was at his restaurant in town. I drove to Tony's restaurant and took a seat at a convenient table, set up my tape recorder, and placed my clipboard directly in front of me. Tony was chatting with some customers and told me that he would be with me shortly. Once I finished setting up, I walked over to his wife, Cathy, who was busy preparing a to-go order for a customer, and greeted her. When his patrons paid their bill and left, Tony joined me at my table. Before I began my interview, I told him the book's premise and I started recording. "A Real Man Stands Tall, an interview with Antonyo Muse. Good afternoon."

"Good afternoon," he replied.

"Let's begin…"

Author: **What was it like growing up with your father?**

Tony: Growing up with my father was strange. The reason I say strange is because there were a lot of things he was trying to instill in us that we didn't understand. Other kids our age were getting into devilment, and we wanted to do those things too. Daddy had a way of talking us out of doing those things. Now that I am a man and I look at those kids who are now grown, I understand and appreciate why he wouldn't allow us to follow the crowd. Many of those same kids that I grew up with are on drugs or in jail or dead. We are better citizens, better men, better husbands, and better fathers because of our parents. My sisters are better women, better wives, and better mothers because of how we were raised.

Author: **What do you admire most about your father?**

Tony: His integrity. He stands for what he believes. Even against opposition, my father stands for what he believes God has told him to do. I admire his devotion to his church and his family. If God would allow me to choose my father, I would select Daniel Muse, Sr. all over again. My father has mentored so many boys who are now men because of his guidance. There aren't a lot of men who can say that. My father is my role model.

Author: **What is the greatest life lesson your father taught you?**

Tony: My father has taught me so many life lessons. It's hard to just speak about one. My father is very giving. He gives of himself to benefit others. He often tells us and the church, "Give and it shall be given unto you…" He has always taught me to treat people the way I want to be treated.

Author: **What has your father taught you about being a man?**

Tony: Now that I am older, my father and I often sit and talk. We have some deep discussions. What I have learned about being a man, I have learned from just watching him. When we were younger, my mother would be at work and my father would get off work before she did. He would pick us up from school and bring us home. We would clean up the house so that mama wouldn't have to come home and clean up. While we would be cleaning up, he would cook us flapjacks. They would be a little on the scorched side, but they would hit the spot nonetheless. My mother worked a lot of nights. My dad trained us how to wash and fold clothes, wash dishes, sweep and mop and wax the floors, dust the furniture, make up our bed, and how to cook. All of us know how to do anything related to keeping a house up. This taught me that a man has to, point blank, be a man.

Author: **Based on your observation of the way your father treats your mother, what have you learned about being a husband?**

Tony: My father, from the way he treats my mother, has taught me how to treat and love a woman. Just from watching my father, I have learned how to be devoted to family. I learned that work is not a choice, it's a must. If a man doesn't work, he doesn't eat! I have seen my parents go out to eat and order one plate of food and share it. The two of them sharing one plate – sometimes feeding each other. That's love. What my father taught me, I am teaching my boys.

Author: **Based on your knowledge of how your father treated you and your siblings, what have you learned about being a father?**

Tony: My father taught me not to have a respecter of persons. Don't have favorites. Don't love one child more than the others. We all had chores. We were all disciplined. As they say, "What's good for the goose is good for the gander." We all had to help out around the house. Both parents and children have responsibilities around the house. I am a better father because of my dad.

Author: **What do you love most about your father?**

Tony: I love the fact that my father is a real man. I have much respect for my father. Although we are all grown up and have our own family, we love spending time with our daddy. We love and respect him to the fullest!

Author: **What is your fondest memory of your father?**

Tony: When I was a young boy, I had a fight with a boy up the street. The boy whooped me and whooped me good. I ran home crying. When I made it home, daddy was outside in the yard. He saw me crying and asked what was wrong. When I told him what had happened to me, he told me that I better go back up that street and not to come home unless I won the fight. I went back up the street and came back home a winner.

Author: **Now that you are a man, a husband, and a father, how has your father's teachings influenced you the most?**

Tony: As long as I can remember, my father has always been about family. He taught me to have balance. Although it is a must that I work, it is a must that I also find time to spend with my family. No matter how exhausted I am, I must spend quality time with my family. I must spend quality time with my wife and quality time with my sons. I can remember when we were younger, every Friday night my father would take us to Burger King. We looked forward to those Friday night dinner dates. I remember my sister, Margaret, used to pluck all the sesame seeds off her burger. When Junior got a little older, we stopped going. I don't know why we stopped going. We had so much fun at Burger King.

Author: **How did the death of Junior affect your family?**

Tony: I was the last person to see Junior alive. I went into his hospital room. He was heavily sedated. I looked at him just laying there. I told him to accept peace and leave the rest up to God.

For a little less than a minute, his breathing became normal. Junior always had problems breathing. He couldn't open his eyes because he was so heavily sedated, but I saw a tear trickle down his face. That tear gave me confirmation that he had accepted what I had said. Not long after that, he passed. His death deeply hurt the family. I am the choir director and organist for the church. My brother Victor is the drummer for the church. My cousin Jarrod plays bass guitar for the church. Junior also played bass guitar for the church. Before Junior died, we had just got our music tight. We planned to do some recording. Once Junior passed, we all felt like giving up music. One service, we all just got on our respective instrument and ministered to the glory of God. This is what Junior would have wanted us to do – continue playing music which we enjoy and love. The power of prayer brought us through that storm.

Author: **It is my understanding that none of y'all have ever been in trouble with the law. Your father has never had to come down to the jailhouse and post bail for any of y'all. Why is that so?**

Tony: Neither I nor my brothers or my sisters are above the law. We were just taught to abide by the law. I can say in the words of Asaph: "But as for me, my feet had almost stumbled; my steps had nearly slipped" (Psalms 73:2). None of us wanted to bring shame upon our church, our family, and especially our father. My father is the founder and pastor of Greater Community Church of God in Christ. He has repeatedly told the youth of the church: "You represent Community. Don't go out in the community and bring shame upon your church." We have always tried to live by that.

Author: **What is your definition of a real man?**

Tony: I am not just saying this because he is my father. Daniel Muse, Sr. is my definition for a real man. From the premise of your book, my father stands tall in his family, in the church, and in the community. My father is not perfect. I have seen his tears. The devil can knock him down, but he can't knock him out. My father is a man of integrity. He will always get up with his integrity intact. Always!

Author: **If your father would be caught up today and taken into heaven, like the Prophet Elijah, but you could have five minutes with him before he would be taken away, what would you say to him?**

Tony: I would congratulate him on a job well done. I would tell him that I love him. I would thank him for all the whuppins I received that I thought I didn't deserve. I would also thank him for making me a better man, husband, and father.

I concluded my interview with Tony, and we talked about the book for a few moments. I told him how impressed I was with his family. I then thanked him for his time and left.

INTERVIEW WITH MARGARET MUSE MITCHELL

When I returned to my car after interviewing Tony, I phoned Margaret to see where she was. She told me that she was at home and that she wasn't feeling well. I told her that I only needed forty-five minutes of her time for the interview. She told me to come on. When I made it to her home, her eldest son, Kedrien, was outside raking the yard. We exchanged greetings and I went inside and set up. We sat at her table. I told her about the book's premise and began recording the interview. "A Real Man Stands Tall, an interview with Margaret Muse."

Author: **What's your relationship like with your father?**

Margaret: I have a great relationship with my father. He is my friend, my buddy, my dad, my confidant, and my pastor. I couldn't ask for a better relationship.

Author: **What do you admire most about your father?**

Margaret: His honesty and his integrity. No matter what the rumors were or what negative words were said about him or what he has gone through, my daddy has always maintained his integrity. He stands by his word.

Author: **How does your father treat your mother?**

Margaret: Like a queen. When I was a little girl, I always told myself that I want a man to treat me the way my father treats my mother.

Author: **As a woman, how does that make you feel?**

Margaret: My father is living proof that all men aren't dogs. As they say, "The proof is in the pudding." My father is proof that a man can be a man and yet, be a gentleman. My father is proof that a man can be a friend to his wife, a confidant to his wife, a counselor to his wife, a lover (although I don't like to think or talk about that part of their marriage) to his wife, and not just a dictator. [I ask: *How do you think you got here? I know you don't believe that myth about the stork delivering babies. We both laugh.*]

Author: **Was your father the template for your selection of a husband?**

Margaret: Yes indeed! As long as I can remember, my father has always been there for us – cooking, cleaning, washing clothes, and bathing us. My dad has even combed my hair. [*She chuckled when she said that. I took that to mean that his styles weren't as nice as her mom's.*] My mom has been there too, but she used to work a lot of evenings. My father has provided for us. Whatever we needed, he was right there to provide it for us – love, spiritual guidance, money, food, clothes, discipline. He was always there. My husband, Bobby, knows he has some big shoes to fill, and he is doing a great job.

Author: **How has your father made an impact on your husband?**

Margaret: My husband didn't grow up with his biological father. He is from Alabama. At the age of seven, his parents divorced and his mother moved them to Hammond, Louisiana. He spent many summers visiting his biological father, but he grew up with his step-father. He has a great relationship with my father.

He calls my father, dad, and my dad treats him like one of his sons.

Author: **In your eyes, how did your father help your family handle the death of Junior?**

Margaret: That's a tough one. Junior's death brought so much hurt and pain. As a young girl, I always believed that if daddy said it would be okay, it would be okay. When Junior passed, I went to my daddy and looked him in his eyes. He held me as I cried in his arms. He held me and told me that it was okay. He just stood there and held me as I cried in his arms, and I knew that everything would be alright. Next to my mom, I know my daddy better than any other woman. My dad was in so much pain. In the midst of his pain, he brought us comfort. In my eyes, that's a real man. Even when he's weak, he's strong.

Author: **What's your favorite pastime with your father?**

Margaret: When I was younger, I used to love when my dad made me flapjacks. Now I just like spending time with him. I enjoy leaving little notes and cards around the house to brighten up his day, to let him know that he is loved and appreciated.

Author: **As a woman, what's your idea of a real man?**

Margaret: A real man must have a relationship with God. He has to be a provider for his family – spiritually, physically, emotionally, and financially. A real man should be strong enough to be weak enough to cry. He must be willing to listen, to hear the cries – concerns – of his family. A real man can take constructive criticism. It makes him a better man.

Author: **Why do you consider your father to be a real man?**

Margaret: Because he is all that and more. I have seen my father take something from nothing and build something great. My father is resilient. He can take a beating, but he won't stay down. He has always been there for his sisters and his brothers. I believe that if they could, they would call him "daddy." He is a rock. That's a real man.

After I ended my interview, we just sat there and talked about the book and what I hoped to accomplish from writing it. I told her that I was deeply moved by her family. I thanked her and told her to get some rest.

INTERVIEW WITH VICTOR MUSE

When I phoned Victor, he was at his parents' house, reclining under the carport. When I arrived at his parents' home, his daughter and nephew were outside playing. Because the children were playing and having fun, he suggested that we sit in his truck to filter the noise from the children playing in the yard. Once inside the truck, we talked about the book's premise and I set up the tape recorder in the center console and placed my clipboard, which contained my questions, in my lap. I started recording and began the interview. "A Real Man Stands Tall, an interview with Victor Muse. Good afternoon."

"Good afternoon," he replied.

Author: **Can you tell me about your relationship with your father?**

Victor: I have a great relationship with my father. Sometimes, he's like a big brother, while other times he is my dad. If I could choose my father, I would choose Daniel Muse, Sr. Our relationship is outstanding. He believes in training up a child in the way he should go. He is approachable and easy to talk to. He is always available to listen when I feel the need to talk. He doesn't meddle in your business; however, he will advise you on your business. He's a father, a big brother, and a friend.

Author: **Is your father your role model?**

Victor: It's funny that you asked me that question. I never saw my father as my role model until a few years ago. We live in a world where everybody wants to be like Mike. One day I began to meditate on my father's life. He took an idea, a vision (against much opposition from the church), and built one of the largest and most successful churches in our community. He is a wonderful husband to my mother and an outstanding father to me, my brothers and sisters. He is the most positive man I know. I see him almost everyday. I know his lifestyle. I know what he stands for. I respect him to the fullest! I would love to be like him. Yes! He is my role model.

Author: **When was the last time your father told you that he loved you?**

Victor: Verbally, it has been awhile; however, he tells me everyday. Every time I am around him, his actions tell me that he loves me. His concern for me and my well-being tells me that he loves me.

Author: **When was the last time you told him that you loved him?**

Victor: I don't tell him as often as I should, but I love him just the same. [*I told Victor that every time my son and I talk or text each other I tell him that I love him. That's how I end the text or conversation. A friend of mine named Edward Slocum, who was a former co-worker and roommate, had a heart attack and died in his sleep at the young age of twenty-two. I never once told him that I loved him. Although I had plenty of opportunities to do so, I never once said those words to him, fearing it would weaken my manhood. He was like a younger brother to me. I regret that I never told him how much he meant to me. That was a great life lesson for me. Now I don't let a day go by without telling my friends and family, when our paths cross, that I love them. It is a good feeling when someone tells you that they love you and it is from the heart.*]

Author: **Have you ever seen your father cry?**

Victor: Yes! The last time I saw my father cry was when someone misconstrued his intentions. When the good that he did for someone was evil spoken of. I have also seen my father cry over the death of a close friend or family member. Junior's death affected him deeply.

Author: **How did seeing your father cry affect you?**

Victor: It affected my deeply. My father only cries when he is heavily burdened. It shows me that he is human, and it hurts because I am helpless. I feel helpless because I know that I can't ease his pain. My father is a pillar of strength. To see him broken humbles me.

Author: **What have you learned from your father about being a man?**

Victor: As a kid, my father always taught me to respect my elders. He taught me to always hold my head up high, always look people in the eye, and stand for what I believe.

Author: **What is your fondest memory of your father?**

Victor: I have many fond memories of my father. If I had to choose one, this would be it. My father, my bother Tony, and I went fishing. My father ain't a fisherman. He has a hard time with casting. He spent more time trying to free his line from the trees than he did fishing. The three of us laughed so much. We had a great time. What impressed me was the fact that I was able to laugh with and at him and he was able to accept my laughter and not be offended. Tony is the fisherman. He showed my father the art of casting. He finally managed to keep his line out of the trees. This showed me that not only is my father a great teacher of God's Word, he is also teachable.

Author: **Now that you are a man, a husband, and a father, how has your father's teachings impacted your life?**

Victor: My father has taught me how to tap into my spiritual and natural side. The bible teaches *first natural, then spiritual*. He has taught me how to love and how to care about others. As I watch him and my mother interact with each other, I learn what it means to be one – unity. They are always in agreement. I was thirty-five when I saw them argue for the first time. Until then, I had no inclination that they had disagreements. I guess my parents are human after all.

Author: **If your father would be caught up today, like the Prophet Elijah, and God gave you five minutes with him before taking him up to Heaven, what would you say to your dad?**

Victor: I would thank him for being my counselor, my leader, my best friend, and my role model. I would thank him for teaching me how to be a real man, how to love my wife, and how to raise a family. Finally, I would say, "I Love You." In fact, he would hear those words until he was caught up into the heavens.

Author: **What's your definition of a real man?**

Victor: A real man is humble, responsible, loving, caring, and teachable. He is humble enough to accept situations that are not within his power to change and strong enough to change the situations that are within the realm of his power. A real man is touchable – he can be moved by the feelings of others. My father is a real man. Thank you for considering my father for your book.

When I concluded my interview with Victor, I was deeply moved by each member of the Muse family. Although I interviewed them all separately and in different locations, I was amazed at how unified their responses were. As a man, I don't quite measure up to the stature of Rev. Muse. I vow to do better. As I shook Victor's hand, exited his truck, and returned to my car, I thanked God for leading me to Greater Community. My heart smiled because I knew that the testimony of the Muse Family would inspire many of the readers of my book to do better, to be better, and to love better! The bible says, "The first shall be made last and the last shall be made first." In the spirit of that statement, I have chosen to put the last season, these interviews, first. I hope you were blessed by the testimonies of Reverend Muse and his family. I also hope you enjoy the rest of the book.

SPRING
ESSAYS

THE ESSENCE OF A REAL MAN

Throughout the years, I've often heard the statement, "A good man is hard to find." Either that is a true statement or you're looking for him in all the wrong places. Perhaps he is right under your nose and you are too blind to notice him because you do not know what a good man looks like. Well, what is a good man, and what are the defining factors that make him such a good man? It is the objective of this paper to reveal the truth that a good man – in all actuality – is a real man, and the essence of a real man is godly character. Character, as defined by Webster's Dictionary, is "The aggregate of features and traits that form the individual nature of a person or thing." In laymen's terms, it is a person's reputation. "Every tree is known by its own fruit" (Luke 6:44a). "A good man out of the good treasure of his heart bringeth forth that which is good" (Luke 45a).

In *Up from Slavery*, the autobiography of Booker T. Washington, Mr. Washington tells the story of an ex-slave who made an agreement with his master to purchase his freedom. He went up North to find work. Periodically, he returned to his master's home to make payments on his agreement. Before he could make his final payments on his freedom, President Lincoln freed the slaves. Although he was a free man, he continued to walk many miles to make payments on his agreement until his final payment was made. When asked why he continued to make payments on his freedom when Lincoln had already freed him, he replied, "I have never broken a promise and I won't start now." In my eyes, this slave was the epitome of a real man. I was taught that a man's word is his bond.

A real man accepts this formula for success: First, I will be a man. Second, I will be a husband. And last, I will be a father. Manhood has its own set of responsibilities which become compounded when a man takes on the role of a husband and / or father. If he goes to stage two – being a husband – before he completes stage one – becoming a man – or if he proceeds to stage three – becoming a father – and bypasses stages one and two, his odds of success are greatly lowered. This is the reality for which many men never take into consideration. Let's explore the responsibilities of each of these stages.

Looking at manhood: Manhood is not measured by how many muscles you can pump up, how many guys you can beat up, or by how many women you can knock-up. Nor is manhood measured by the size, or lack thereof, of a man's penis. If that were the case, there are a lot of teenage boys who could unzip their pants and give many adult males a run for their money. Does that fact make these boys men? I was raised to believe that a boy becomes a man when he is able to stand on his own two feet – accept and handle responsibility. This includes, but it is not limited to, caring and providing for himself. My grandmother used to say, "Every tub has got to sit on its own bottom." Based on that theory, there are many adult males who haven't made the transition from boyhood to manhood. I have known of quite a few men who rely on their moms or ole ladies to provide their basic needs as well as many of their wants. Many of them lounge around the house watching television, talking on the phone, or playing video games while their mom or ole lady is at work. A real man would never allow himself to be financially dependent on any woman – mother, wife, girlfriend, aunt, grandmother, sister, et cetera – unless he had some mental or physical disability that prevented him from working. A real man knows the reality that if he doesn't work, he won't eat or be able to meet his financial obligations; therefore, he maintains a stable and solid work history.

As a husband, a real man accepts and handles the responsibility of being the head of his wife. He is fully aware that this position is not a dictatorship. His wife is not his servant, his slave, or his doormat. She is his helpmeet – companion and helper. Husband and wife are co-laborers – they work together as a team. A real man knows that if he is king of his castle, his wife is the queen. Everyone knows that a queen is worthy of just as much honor and respect as a king; therefore, she must be treated with such. If both husband and wife work full-time jobs, they share the workload at home. A real man knows how to cook, clean, and do laundry.

He may not enjoy doing it, but he does know how to do it! If a man can keep his automobile (something that he only rides in) immaculate, he can also keep his home (a place where both he and his family eat, live, and rest their heads) just as clean.

Contrary to popular opinion, housework is not woman's work. It is teamwork – a shared responsibility. I once heard a man say, "This is my house! I wear the pants in my house! At my house, I am the boss!" My response to such an ignorant, lame statement: Since it is your house, wash your dishes, cook your food, vacuum, sweep and mop your floors! Make up your bed, wash, dry, fold, and put away your clothes! It's only right since it is your house! I can appreciate those households that have the understanding that the man takes care of the automobiles, yard, inside and outside maintenance – upkeep of the home and cars – while the woman takes care of the inner running of the home; however, a real man can run everything in his house – the lawnmower, dishwasher, washer and dryer, vacuum cleaner – and he can cook. According to celebrity chef Emeril Lagasse, author of *Real Men Cook*, some of the best cooks in this world are men.

A real man also knows that his wife is human. She gets tired too! Therefore, he loves her like Christ loves His church. She is his crown and not someone to be taken for granted. Before I move on, allow me to add this: If a woman has chosen the option to be a housewife, it is her duty, responsibility, and job to keep the house clean, minister to the needs of her husband and children, and prepare the family meals. Her man who goes to work each day to provide for his family should never come home to a dirty house, dirty kids, or a foodless stove, unless she (his woman) is ill or sick.

Now as a father, a real man steps up to the plate and takes care of business. He knows that his children are his legacy. Therefore, he must "bring them up in the admonition of the Lord" (Ephesians 6:4). His blood flows through their veins. He plays a major role in their success and / or failure. A real man realizes the fact that many families have been destroyed or left handicapped by generational curses; therefore, he's not satisfied with being the missing link in the lives of his children. He knows that he must play a positive, active role in their lives. He's also aware that his sons may some day follow in his footsteps. It's his responsibility to mold and shape them into men by setting a good example for them to follow. As they say, like father, like son. A real man doesn't live by the old adage, "Do as I say, not as I do." He knows the importance of leading by example. Actor Will Smith, speaking in reference to his children in an interview with JET magazine said, "The best thing that you can be is an example. I just feel it's my responsibility." He could have not been more right. But in order to be an example for your son, you must spend quality time with him –depositing wisdom, knowledge, instruction, and understanding into his heart. That's the true love of a father.

A real man is also cognizant of the fact that he sets the stage for what type of men his daughters will get involved with. He's aware of the hypothesis that many women are attracted to men who remind them of their fathers. When Coretta Scott was dating Martin Luther King, Jr., she often said to him, "You remind me so much of my father." A real man knows the importance of sowing the right seeds into his daughters' lives so that he can reap a better harvest. Allow me to give you an example of what I am saying. There is a man whom I highly esteem and admire. He has a beautiful wife and three lovely daughters – daddy's girls. At the time of this writing, he had no sons. He treats his girls like princesses; however, he doesn't spoil them. Would you eat food that is spoiled? If not, why would you spoil your children? When something is spoiled, it is no longer fit to be used for its intended purpose. Just because he wants the best for his daughters and exposes them to the finer things in life, it doesn't mean they will be spoiled. He teaches them respect for self and others, and if they get out of line, he is quick to correct them. "Spare the rod, spoil the child" (Proverbs 13:24).

He takes every opportunity to show them how a real man is supposed to treat a woman – a lady. He buys them nice clothes, nice things, and takes them to some of the finest restaurants. He doesn't want his daughters to settle for fast food dining – the typical dinner location for other guys. He treats his wife – their mother – like the queen that she is. He teaches his daughters to expect the same royal treatment from the men they choose to date and / or marry. Both he and his wife, if they have a disagreement, refuse to argue in front of their daughters. He never strikes or hits their mother because real men don't hit or beat women. He doesn't want his daughters to accept physical abuse from any man. Their mother wouldn't tolerate it and neither should they! Besides, they were not raised in an abusive environment. Allow me to add this: When his wife speaks about him, she says the most amazing, wonderful things about him as both a husband and father. I have never witnessed a woman speaking so highly of her man before. These days, all you hear are women talking badly about their baby's daddy. But it is so refreshing, uplifting, and encouraging to know that there are some real men holding it down.

In conclusion, a certain ruler approached Jesus saying, "Good Master, what shall I do to inherit eternal life?" Jesus replied, "Why callest thou me good? None is good, save one, that is God" (Luke 18:19). Jesus wanted the young man to know that by calling someone good meant that he recognized the presence of God in that individual's life; therefore, a good man is not only a real man but also a godly man. A real man accepts and strives to live by the principles of God – God's Word. Although he isn't perfect, that doesn't discourage him from striving for perfection. He won't make excuses for his failures or shortcomings. A real man makes choices, not mistakes. He knows that life is sculptured by our choices. When you say that you made a mistake, you fail to take responsibility for your actions. When you admit that you made a choice, you take full responsibility for your actions. Real men welcome responsibility. A real man is fully aware of his strengths as well as his weaknesses. Whatever capacity – bachelor, husband, father – life grants him, he fulfills that role to the best of his abilities. "In all his ways, he acknowledges the Lord and allows Him to direct his paths" (Proverbs 3:6). A Real Man realizes the fact that "The steps of a good man are ordered by the Lord" (Psalms 37:23).

FORGIVENESS: GOD'S PRESCRIPTION FOR HEALING

It is very ironic that we enter this world crying. We cry at the beginning of life (birth); we cry at different seasons in life; and we cry when life is coming or has come to an end (death). Babies cry, children cry, teenagers cry, and even adults cry. Some fool once said, "A man ain't supposed to cry." Men do cry – some may not want to admit that they cry, but they do! There are countless reasons why we shed tears and cry. One of the main reasons why tears flow from our eyes is because we are hurting or have been hurt. When someone has wronged or injured us, our natural instinct is to retaliate – hurt back. Usually, we want them to feel what we are feeling, to experience our hurt and pain; however, that's not God's remedy for healing. Forgiveness is God's prescription for healing.

In order for the healing process to begin, we must first learn how to forgive. Then, we must learn to forgive. "And when ye stand praying, forgive, if you have ought against any that your Father also which is in heaven may forgive you your trespasses" (Mark 11:25). Webster defines forgiveness as *the act of forgiving or the state of being forgiven.* According to Webster, to forgive means *to pardon an offense or an offender and to cease to feel resentment against.* As a youth, I was constantly told, "To err is human, but to forgive is divine." That sounds good, but what does it really mean and is it easy to do? My grandmother often said, "Baby, you'll understand it better by and by." It amazes me how time has a unique way of answering life's most perplexing questions. When Jesus was dying on the cross, He looked up to heaven and said, "Father, forgive them for they know not what they do" (Luke 23:34). If He wanted to, Jesus could have commanded angels to descend from heaven and consume His persecutors. Instead, He asked

His father to forgive them. Allow me to digress for a moment. When I was a teenager, I watched a movie entitled, *Mandingo*. In the movie, a Black slave was being hung. As he was being hung from a tree, he looked at his captors and told each of them to kiss his gluteus maximus. That's not the phrase he used. But I know you know what I'm talking about. What a striking contrast between Jesus and the Negro slave. Both were being hung. But why did Jesus choose to forgive rather than to curse his persecutors? Because Jesus knew that forgiveness is God's prescription for healing.

While attending Greater Antioch Full Gospel Baptist Church in New Orleans on Sunday, April 8, 2001, the pastor (Elder Lester Love) preached a very powerful message entitled, *Releasing the Anger*. Forgiveness was the foundation upon which the message was constructed. In Pastor Love's message, he told the congregation something along these lines: "A close relative came into your room one night and molested you as a child, and you never told anyone." As he continued uttering offenses that people within the congregation may have experienced, he said, "Your father walked out on you years ago, and you are still angry with him." As Pastor Love spoke on, conviction inundated my heart. As a youth, I cried myself to sleep longing for my father's hand to guide me. When I became a man, I blamed my father for everything that had gone wrong in my life. Let me explain my reasons for holding my father accountable.

Like most young boys, I loved and looked up to my father. In my eyes, although I was naïve, my father could do no wrong. My parents were teenage sweethearts. My mother married my father when she was seventeen years old. My father was both verbally and physically abusive to my mother; therefore, she asked him for a separation. Years later, they divorced. Although my mother divorced him, I did not. He was no longer my mother's husband; however, he was still my dad. In fact, I look just like my father. Besides, I am named after him – James Jr. Since he was still my father, I had aspirations of continuing my relationship with him. Because of these grand illusions, I had a hard time understanding why I hardly ever saw my father. Why didn't he come around more often? Why didn't he show up on Christmas Day or my birthday bearing gifts of goodwill? Did he love or even care about me and my wellbeing? These were perplexing questions that plagued my childhood. They caused me much anguish, grief, pain, and many sleepless nights.

Was it wrong for me to believe that my father had a responsibility to provide for and protect us – his family? What about the vow he made to love, honor, and cherish my mother until death due them part? Was it wrong for me to believe that he was supposed to hold fast to those vows he made in the sight of God? Maybe I was just naïve. I honestly believed that his duty was to bring home the bacon, so that my mom could fry the bacon, and so that we could eat the bacon. I was under the impression that he was supposed to take an active role in our lives and to correct or chastise us when we were unruly, disobedient, disrespectful, or mischievous. I didn't know that beating my mother was part of the deal.

As a husband and father, he failed miserably! In spite of that, my love for him did not cease. Although I did not condone his actions and behavior, I did love my father. Children love because of and in spite of. That's unconditional love. I didn't ask much of him. All I required of him was his love and presence. It really didn't matter what he could give me financially. I just wanted him to be a part of my life. Was that too much to ask? Time and attention, to me, are both priceless.

When I was sixteen, years after my parents' divorce, I was afforded the opportunity to go and live with my father. Like a kid on Christmas Day, I was ecstatic. My dream of being closer to my dad had finally come to fruition. I had nothing against my mother. I just wanted a closer relationship with my dad; therefore, I moved in with him and his common-law wife, Rose, and finished my junior year at Hammond High School. I lived with my father for about seven months. In those seven months, he stole money from me once and continued to break promise after promise. I am very grateful God granted me the opportunity to get to know my father by living with him. As they say, "You never truly know a person until you live with them." Had I not gone and lived with my father, I would be living in a state of limbo – fantasizing about what it would have been like to grow up with my father. Because he was not my legal guardian, I wasn't allowed to re-enroll at Hammond High and complete my senior year. I had to move back in with my mom and her new husband and finish my senior year at Independence High School. I am very grateful that I returned to live with my mother and had the pleasure of attending Independence High School. My senior year was amazing!

Six months after I graduated from high school, my mom gave me the down payment and co-signed for my first car. I remember that day as if it were yesterday. My mom and I walked into Citizen's National Bank, in Amite, Louisiana. My mom told them that she wanted to apply for a car loan. Mr. Dees, the vice-president of the bank, invited her to have a seat in his office to discuss the loan, while I anxiously waited outside. I would like you to know that my mom had weak credit, but strong faith! She is a woman of great prayer. After they had been talking for a while, Mr. Dees motioned for me to come into his office. He said, "Young man, your mother speaks very highly of you. She tells me that you graduated from high school with honors and after you graduated, you found a job and went straight to work. She tells me that you are planning on going to college. You have no credit, but because your mother speaks so highly of you, I am willing to take a chance on you. I am approving your loan. Good luck, young man, with college. Don't let me down." He then called the dealership where I had picked out my car and told them that my loan was approved. He told them to let me have the car and send him all the paperwork. He then shook my hand and said, "Young man, go pick up your new car." What a contrast between my father and my mother. My mother always kept her word and made good on her promises.

I went to Dixie Motors in Hammond and picked up my new car. I was elated! One day I decided to taunt my dad. I drove by his house and stopped at the corner, a few yards from his doorsteps. I began honking my horn. When he came to the door, I yelled, "See what my mom and my real dad bought me?" Profanity spewed out of his mouth along with threats. My dad could be a very violent man when provoked or angered; therefore, I jumped back in my car and sped off. Later, I told my mom about the incident. I told her that if my car would have stalled, I would have left it on that corner and ran home – all fifteen miles! We both laughed.

Two years after I graduated from high school, I moved to New Orleans. My dad and I had developed a speaking relationship by this time – we talked whenever our paths crossed. About two years or so after I moved to New Orleans, I applied for admission to the University of New Orleans (UNO) and was accepted. When my father heard that I was preparing to go to college, he informed me that he wanted to help with my tuition. That sounds nice doesn't it? Apparently, you don't know my father like I had grown to know him. Because he had broken every promise he had ever made to me, I told him that wasn't necessary. He became adamant and convinced me that he sincerely wanted to help with my tuition. Reluctantly, I accepted his offer. He gave me a day and a time to come by the house to pick up the money.

When the day arrived for me to go and get the money from my father, I had mixed emotions. Was my father really going to help pay my college tuition? Was he trying to change his ways and make amends for all his wrongs in regards to me? I gave him the benefit of the doubt. I arrived at his home and knocked on the door. Since no one answered, I continued to knock. Still, no one answered my knock at the door. I could not believe this. He knew I was coming because he told me to come. I turned the doorknob and, to my surprise, the door was unlocked. Because I used to reside there, I went in. As I walked through the house, I called out to him. Again, no one answered. Just as I figured. Another empty promise. Weeks later, my dad's common-law wife, Rose, told me that he was home that day I came by and no one answered the door when I knocked. She said, "Lil James, his big ass was hiding in the closet." That was the straw that broke the camel's back. I made myself a vow. I would never again give my father the opportunity to disappoint me. On that day, my love for him soured. I had nothing but animosity, contempt, and disgust for my father. At that time, I could honestly say that I hated my father; however, as the years progressed, my feelings went from hate to pity. I neither loved nor hated him. On the contrary, I felt sorry for him.

Finally, Pastor Love concluded his message. At the conclusion of his message, he extended an altar call for all those individuals who had been wounded by someone in their past and who needed to forgive the perpetrator – to release the anger, hurt, and pain. I realized that the time had finally come for me to forgive my father of all the bad choices he had made in regards to his family and his obligations to his family. Therefore, I went to the altar to release it – surrender the anger, hurt, and pain, to God. I was determined to take my burdens to the Lord and to leave them there – at the altar. It was at that moment that I realized that anger, bitterness, and resentment were all cancerous to my soul. A heart that refuses to forgive is like a cancerous cell. In order for God to heal my wounded spirit and mend my broken heart, I had to forgive my father. Minister and inspirational author Catherine Ponder once said, "Forgiveness is all-powerful. It heals all ills."

In conclusion, writer and literary critic Joseph Jacobs said, "Forgiveness is the highest and most difficult of all moral lessons." Sometimes it is a pill that's hard to swallow or a step that's hard to make. However, it is a step that must be taken if you have any hopes of walking with God. When I left that altar, I felt liberated! Empowered! Although my father was deceased, I thanked him for being the instrument God used to grant me life. Let's face the facts: I wouldn't be here if it wasn't for him. My mother could not have conceived without my father's deposit. Believe it or not, my father taught me numerous valuable lessons. For that, I am eternally grateful. I will be a better man, a better husband, and a better father as long as I do not walk in my father's footsteps. I realize that we have the most to gain when we choose to forgive. According to renowned Italian psychiatrist Robert Assaglioli, "Without forgiveness, life is governed ... by an endless cycle of resentment and retaliation." You must break the cycle and forgive. If you don't, you will never know personal peace.

"And, ye fathers, provoke not your children to wrath: but bring them up in the nurture and admonition of the Lord" (Ephesians 6:4). Fathers, you have been mandated by God to provide your children with the basic necessities – financial support, emotional support, physical support, and spiritual support – that will enrich their lives and allow them to grow up and become responsible and productive adults. Child support is more than a monthly check that you have been ordered to pay by the court system. We (your sons) need you (our fathers) to take an active role in our lives and help us make the transition from boys to men – real men! And to those fathers who choose not to take an active role in our lives: we forgive you.

THE POWER OF MENTORING: AN EARTH ANGEL NAMED, "GOO"

Alpha: March 29, 1957 – Omega: May 11, 2016

Growing up without a father created an abyss in my life. There were many days and nights I found myself wiping tears from my eyes as I pondered thoughts of my father. I don't have many fond memories of activities shared with my dad. I have some but not many. I wish I could boast about memories of me and my dad tossing around a football, playing catch with a baseball, flying a kite, going fishing, pillow fighting, or even partaking in a father-and-son picnic. Now that I have had time to think on the subject, I don't have one single memory of my father tickling me on the bed or floor, while I laugh hysterically. I realize that these things may seem petty; however, to a growing, impressionable boy, they mean the world. I believe activities like these solidify the bond shared between a father and his son. They create memories that leave footprints on a boy's heart.

Although I don't have many positive memories of me and my father, I have a plethora of memories of an angel named Goo. He was my mentor. Growing up in the 70s and early 80s, I had no conception of who or what a mentor was or did, for that matter. But as I look back in time through the bifocals of hindsight, what I knew in part, I now know in full. God supplied me with a "ram in the bush." He placed a young man in my life who would serve as both a big brother and surrogate father to me. His name is Lawrence "Goo" Harrison.

I grew up on Myrtle Street, in Amite, Louisiana. The part of town where I was raised is called Butler Town. Goo also lived on Myrtle Street.

He was a student at Southern University (SU) in Baton Rouge, Louisiana. His major was Education. Goo had aspirations of being a teacher. Little did we neighborhood kids know – and neither did Goo – we would be his first pupils, his first classroom. Like typical kids, we loved to play and have fun. Our favorite pastime was playing stickball. Stickball is the ghetto version of baseball. In order to play stickball, you need a stick to serve as a bat and a plastic or rubber ball. Often, we would break off the head of a broom or mop and use the handle (stick) for our bat. The street was our baseball field. We would use whatever was available to lay down in the street to serve as bases. Whenever we played stickball in the street, we would always play in front of Goo's mother's house. Many times, he would come outside and watch us play. I guess he was our guardian angel – watching out for us to make sure we didn't get hit by a car or something of that nature.

Goo was cooler than kool-aid. He had a dog named Chico. Chico would watch over Goo, while Goo watched over us. No matter what was on Goo's agenda, he always found time to spend with the kids in his neighborhood. He took us to the park to play basketball. He loved to jog. Sometimes he would allow us to jog alongside him and engage him in conversation. We would laugh and talk about everything. Many nights, Goo would take us for a ride through the neighborhood in his car. Some nights he would allow us to ride on the hood of his car while he drove slowly through the neighborhood. A few nights, he would drive through the graveyard, stop the car, and then turn off his ignition and head lights. Man, it was so funny to see who would be the first person to run out of the graveyard, screaming! Those were some fun times.

In a nearby town called Hammond, there was a drive-in movie theater. On occasion, Goo would take us there to see a karate movie. I am not sure whether or not you have had the pleasure of going to a drive-in movie theater. Eating popcorn in the car while watching a movie in an open field is so exhilarating! Until you see Bruce Lee kick butt on the big screen while sitting in the front or back seat or on top of the hood of your car, you can't begin to imagine how exciting that was for me.

As I said earlier, Goo was an Education major at Southern University. For one of his class projects, he had to teach some kids a few African games and bring them to class with him to demonstrate what he had taught them. He chose three boys from the block to be his pupils. Of course, I was one of the boys he selected to participate in his class project. I was happy to oblige Goo and be his guinea pig. I was a good student, and Goo was an excellent teacher. Even though this was in the late 70s, I can still vaguely remember one of the games he taught us.

When it came time for us to go to Southern with Goo and demonstrate what we had learned, the other two boys got cold feet and chickened out. Goo had never let us down; therefore, I refused to let him down. Unlike the other two boys, I was ready to get my shine on. After all, this was a big part of Goo's grade. He was counting on me to bring my A game. I was prepared. I was always a ham for the spotlight. I welcomed the challenge. In fact, there was no doubt in my mind that Goo would get an A on his project. He was a good teacher and I was a good student; therefore, the results had to be good.

Goo set up the props while I stood in front of the class and watched with great anticipation. When he finished setting up, he asked, "Are you ready?" I looked at him and smiled. Showtime! I showed out. Goo was thrilled. He received an A on his project. Like a father proud of his son, Goo was very proud of me. He then asked us if we were hungry. When have you known teenage boys to turn down free food? We said, "Yeah!" He took us to Church's Chicken. How ironic is that! The other two boys chickened out, and we all ate chicken afterwards.

Goo was always there for us. Even when he got married, he never turned his back on us. I can remember many Sunday afternoons where my friends and I chilled in Goo's living room to watch the Pittsburgh Steelers play the Dallas Cowboys. I was a big Steelers fan and my friends were fans of the Cowboys; therefore, you can imagine the pandemonium in Goo's living room, especially when the Steelers and the Cowboys faced off in the Super Bowl. Goo's beautiful wife didn't mind sharing her living room with us. In fact, she would fix refreshments for us to snack on while we yelled and screamed at the TV. She was very supportive of her husband and didn't mind sharing him with us. She knew how important we were to him and vice versa.

In summary, Goo was my role model growing up. I can't speak for the other boys. I can only speak on my behalf. He was the most positive male I knew the years of my boyhood. Even when he graduated from Southern, he was still accessible to me. An African proverb says; *It takes a village to raise a child.* This still rings true today. Parents shouldn't have to bear the burden of raising their children alone. Especially single or divorced mothers raising their sons with little to no help from the fathers. They should welcome help from the community, church, and school system. When a boy becomes disobedient, unruly, and delinquent, the entire village is at risk. Like a rabid dog infected with a contagious virus, this troubled boy can contaminate other boys and cause great harm to the village, the community. By reaching out to this boy through the medium of mentoring, you could save his life and the lives of those he may potentially harm if you make a positive impact on his life and intervene. This is the power of mentoring. Tony Dungy, the former head coach for the Indianapolis Colts, said in an interview with *Black Enterprise*: "I know the impact mentors had on my life. I heard a lot of things from my parents but you don't always listen to your mom and dad when you're younger. And a lot of other people need to come into your life and help you."

See, it does take a whole village to raise a child. I don't know what path my life may have taken had not God placed Goo in my life to serve as my mentor – role model. But I do know that I will never forget Goo – my earth angel.

REAL TALK

As I walk downtown on Canal Street in New Orleans, I see a familiar face walking towards me. Seeing that I haven't seen this individual in quite a while, I smile at the sight of him. My smile evokes the same reaction from him when he recognizes me. When we get within arm's reach, we fist-pound and engage in conversation. "What's up Mike- Mike?" I ask.

"It's all good, Jay dawg. What's up witcha?" he responds.

"I'm blessed! Trying to do my thang as a writer. I wrote a book that will be published soon."

"Dat's what's up! Congratulations! I wisha all the best of luck witcha book."

"Thanks! So what's poppin'?"

"Dawg, you don't wanna know. If I toldcha, it might ruin your day."

"Come on Mike-Mike. You know me better than that. I don't let the devil steal my joy. Besides, I don't give any man power over my day or my attitude. It takes more muscles and energy to frown than it does to smile. Therefore, I keep a smile on my face and have a positive attitude. If you wanna talk, I got time if you do. I'm a good listener, and I'm known for dishing out good advice."

"Nah, dawg. I'm good. Besides, I don't wanna burden you wit' my troubles. I'm sure you got yo' own problems ta worry 'bout."

"See! That's our problem. We think it's a sign of weakness when we go to one of our brothers when we are troubled. Women recognize the power of sisterhood. When they are going through something, they don't have a problem confiding in one another. They welcome advice, words of comfort, and support from their sisters. We, on the other hand, think that we are being tough when we keep our problems to ourselves. What are brothers – dawgs – for if you can't go to them and confide in them? Aren't we supposed to have each other's back – be there for each other through thick and thin? Plus, you don't know who your true friends are until you go through something."

"Dat's some real shit! I feel ya' on dat. Jay dawg, I fa'got how smart yo' ass is. You still in church?"

"Now Mike, why you wanna play a brotha like that? If I leave the church, where am I going to go?"

"Come on Jay baby! You know how we are – in today, out tomorrow."

I smile as he makes that comment. "You're right about that! But God has been too good to me for me to turn my back on Him. He brought me from a mighty long way. He knows my whole story and He still loves me. Anyway, what's going on?"

"Shit! A bunch of bullshit! Baby-mama drama."

"It can't be all that bad."

"Dawg, dis girl is drivin' me crazy. Givin' me da blues."

"I had an unction that a woman was at the heart of your troubles. I'm hungry! Do you want to go and get something to eat while we talk about what's on your mind? My treat!" He starts to laugh and says, "You musta heard my stomach growlin'." Smiling I say, "Come on. I know the perfect spot. Let's walk to The Gazebo Café over on Decatur Street."

As we walk through Jackson Square, chatting and taking in the sights, I see an artist friend of mine. She is busy drawing a guy's portrait. Her name is Jemu. She is by far one of the best, if not the best, artist in the square. I let her draw a portrait of me, on two separate occasions. She gives you three options: pencil, black and white, or color. I kid you not when I tell you that my portraits look like photographs. Actually, I look better on the drawings than I do in real life. She's just that good! I say hello to her and we continue walking to the café.

When we arrive at the café, we take a seat at a table, far away from the house band, so that we wouldn't have a problem hearing each other when we talk. When the waitress comes to our table, I order a catfish platter with a glass of lemonade and he orders a seafood platter with a coke. I look at Mike and ask, "What's going on?"

"It's like dis Jay dawg. Me and my baby mama broke up 'bout four months ago. We have a son tagheter; therefore, we still have dealings."

"What do you mean when you say dealings?"

"Come on Jay baby! I nevah took ya fa being green befo'. What do ya thank it means?"

"What do I *think* it means?"

"Dat's what I axed."

"I don't know. That's why I'm asking you. Many words in the English vocabulary are ambiguous. They have more than one meaning. I don't want to assume anything. That's why I want you to tell me what you mean when you use the word."

"A'ight Jay baby. I feel ya on dat. Me and my baby mama are cool. Every now and then, I hit it."

"So the two of you are still sexually involved?"

Smiling from ear-to-ear, he says, "I've been known ta make a booty call or two on a few occasions."

"Are the two of you planning on reconciling and raising your son as a family?"

"Nah dawg. I just got it like dat. I've moved on."

"I can't tell. If you have moved on, then why are you still sleeping with your ex, making deposits and withdrawals in her vault?"

"Who said I was sleeping there? I sex her up and den go ta my own house ta sleep. You see Jay, when I call ta see how my son is doin', she always invites me ovah ta see him. When I get dere, one thang leads ta anotha and we end up havin' sex. I'm sorry Jay dawg! My nature won't allow me ta walk away from free pooh-nanny."

"Mike, don't you realize that nothing in this world is free? Salvation ain't even free! It cost Jesus His life. Drama is the price you pay for sleeping with an ex that you no longer love. Don't you know that men have sex and women make love? Each time you hit it, as you say, you plant seeds of false hope. Meaning, you give her a reason to believe that the two of you will get back together. When she realizes that you truly don't want her, you will have to be a man and take your licks. You will have to deal with a woman that's been scorned."

"I'm dealing wit' dat ret now. I'm only sleeping wit' her so dat she want put me on child support."

"Did I hear you correctly? Your booty calls with the mother of your son are just to pacify her so that she won't place you in the system?"

Smiling, he then says, "Fa da most part. But don't worry, I get me."

"What about the well-being of your son? It seems to me that while you are so busy doing you, your son is getting lost in the shuffle."

"Don't get it twisted Jay dawg. I break bread wit' her. I give her a l'il sump'in sump'in on occasions."

"Mike, I'm glad I ran across you today. The Lord works in mysterious ways."

"Why ya say dat?"

"I'm about to break it down to you. The title of my book is *A Real Man Stands Tall*. The sole purpose of the book is to minister to fathers and sons. You see, the spirit of the father is transferred into his son. That's why they say, 'Like father, like son.' I know you are aware that the apple doesn't fall too far from the tree."

"Yeah! My mama told me dat befo' when she said dat I was just like my dad."

The waitress brings our food and sets it down in front of us. We thank her and I bless the food. I look at Mike and say, "Mike, you may not agree with me, but my words are like castor oil. They won't taste good, but if you swallow them – take my advice – they will do you a lot of good."

"Run it"

"It's like this. A real man will not play with a woman's heart – toy with her emotions. It's evident that your son's mother still has feelings for you. If she isn't wife material, you need to be open and honest with her. You need to let her know that what the two of you once shared is over. The two of you need to focus your attention and energy on raising your son to be the best that he can be by setting a good example for him. You need to free her heart so that she can find and love a man that will reciprocate the love she has to give. How's your food?"

"It's straight. I hear whatcha sayin', but what do I do if she wants ta hold on ta da past?"

"You have to be a man and stop having sex with her. She'll never let go of the past if you keep sleeping with her in the present. You are sending her conflicting messages, saying one thing and doing another."

"Dat's easier said dan done."

"Not really. All you have to do is make up in your mind that you are going to do right by your child and his mother. There's nothing a man can't achieve or accomplish when he makes up his mind and purposes it in his heart."

"I feel ya on dat."

At this time, the waitress brings us a refill on our drinks and I tell her that she can bring us the check. Once I take a sip of my lemonade, I say, "I want to discuss something you said earlier."

"What's dat Jay dawg?"

"You said that you occasionally break bread with your son's mother. Can I ask you a few questions?"

"Go ahead. Speak yo' mind."

"Does your son eat and drink milk only on occasion? Does he occasionally wear pampers and clothes? Does he occasionally need daycare and a roof over his head? Do the gas, lights, and water occasionally come on?"

"I see where ya goin' wit' dis."

"That's the problem. I don't think you see the picture clearly. Your son needs consistency in his life. He won't benefit from you hitting and missing. He needs to learn at an early age that he can count on – depend on – his dad to supply his needs. You must be a vital source of strength in his life. This is paramount! How will he become a man if you are not there to teach him, transfer your spirit into him?"

"My dad wasn't there for me," Mike says, looking me straight in my eyes. "But I feel where ya comin' from. I nevah really thought about it like dat befo'."

"What you do with your life is your business. However, when you bring a child into this world, everything changes. You have to put the needs and welfare of your child above and before your own. You have to make sacrifices for the benefit of your child. I'm not saying that you have to neglect yourself. However, don't do you, at the expense of your child. When it comes to raising children, you have to be selfless, not selfish."

"Dat's real talk. No one has evah broke it down ta me like dat befo'. Dat's why you are my dawg. I thought being a man means dat I can do whatevah I wanna do."

"Not really, Mike. Being a man means accepting and handling responsibility to the best of your abilities. It means that you are willing to accept the responsibility to protect and provide for your family, if you choose to have a family."

"What if I don't know how to provide fa' a family or be a father?"

"Mike, there's no shame in not knowing. The shame is in not wanting to know, not seeking out knowledge and instruction that's readily available. The dumbest question is the one that you never ask. Are you in church?"

"Jay dawg, I can't tell ya da last time I saw da inside of a church."

"What you need to do is find you a good church home and look at the life of the pastor. Examine how he treats his wife and children. Observe how his family interacts with him. Do they support him by working alongside him in ministry? When he preaches, are they in agreement with what he is saying? If you are pleased with your observations, set up an appointment for counseling with the pastor and be open, honest, with him.

"Jay, I believe da Lord sentcha ta minister ta me. Excuse my French. You got some shit witcha!"

"Is that good or bad?"

"Trust me! It's good."

"No doubt. Let me give you my number and get yours so that we can keep in touch this time."

"Fa' sho! Good lookin' out."

"Since we are finished eating and talking, let's stop by Café Du Mond and pick up two orders of beignets. That'll be our desert." Mike smiles and says, "Afta dat seafood platter, I can go fa sump'in sweet ret now." I pay the bill and leave the waitress a ten-dollar tip. We get up from the table and leave, walking towards Café Du Mond.

"Jay dawg, I appreciatecha lookin' out fa a brotha. If ya evah need me, don't hesatate ta call me. I gotcha! Balieve dat! I will also check out dat church. I kno' where it is. Also, let me kno' when yo' book comes out. I wanna buy one and getcha ta autograph it."

"You got that. Now let's get those beignets."

After we eat our beignets and talk briefly, we dap off, hug, vow to keep in touch with each other, and go our separate ways. I'm smiling as I walk towards my car. I feel good about myself. Real good! Real talk!

A TRIBUTE TO MY DAD, JIM JACKSON: A REAL MAN

Alpha: March 29, 1937 – Omega: September 27, 2006
By: Elroy Jackson

On Tuesday, September 26, 2006, my dad and I were working and talking in the field when I received a call on my cell phone from my cousin. My cousin informed me that he was writing a book to minister to fathers and sons. He said that many men were neglecting their responsibilities to their children, especially to their sons; therefore, he was writing this book with the hope of inspiring men to be better fathers. He told me that his book was entitled, A *Real Man Stands Tall*. The reason he called me was because he had an idea to enhance his book. He wanted his book to include a son's tribute to his father, to serve as a testimonial of a real man. Since he felt that his father, my deceased uncle – my mother's brother – wasn't an example of a real man and my dad was, he wanted me to write a tribute to my dad to honor him as a real man. I can't think of a time when my dad wasn't there for me, my mother, my brothers, and my sisters; therefore, I told my cousin that I would do it. I told him that I would need some time to collect my thoughts. The very next day after my cousin's phone call, my dad died of a heart attack. I consider it an honor to write this tribute to my dad, Jim Jackson – a real man.

My dad was the second son born to Alexander and Emma Jackson. He was one of seven boys. He grew up in Wilmer, Louisiana. My dad was raised in a home that was full of love and respect for one another. He had an unbreakable bond with his brothers – my uncles. To say that my dad and uncles were tight would be an understatement. My grandfather (his dad) raised him and my uncles to be men of integrity and honor. He taught them the true meaning of family. My grandfather taught them that faith and trust in God is the glue that binds family together. What his dad taught him, he passed on to his own family. My dad raised me to know that strong values and good morals would take me a long way and guide me through this journey we call life.

At an early age, I knew the importance of family. My dad taught me the family that prays together stays together. God must be the head of your family if you want your family to be a success. I did not always understand why my daddy and momma did some of the things they did. Now that I am older and a parent myself, I understand all too well. We may not always understand the lessons that our parents try to teach us, but as the old saints would say, "You'll understand it better by and by." So many times when I am interacting with my family, I find myself acting and sounding just like my dad. He showed me, through his example, how to be a real man, a loving husband, and a good father. I truly believe God placed my daddy in my life to be my role model. I could not have had a better role model.

I loved watching my dad and mom interact with each other. Although my dad was more of the outdoors kind of guy, he didn't mind helping my mom wash dishes and clean up the kitchen. He believed that if she could labor in the kitchen, preparing meals for the family, the least he could do was help her clean it up after the family had finished eating. Many nights my dad would say to my mom, "Honey, are you ready to straighten up the kitchen?" Like a knight escorting his fair maiden off into the sunset, my dad and mom would be joking and smiling all the way to the kitchen.

Even though my mom did the vast majority of the cooking, my dad could cook a mean pot of red beans. In fact, he had a special pot which he used to cook and simmer his world famous red beans. At family holiday gatherings, my dad took great pride in frying the turkey. He enjoyed the numerous compliments he received from both family and friends about his red beans and fried turkey. Every first Sunday at our church, I, along with two other brothers, cook breakfast for the congregation. On Annual Days and special programs at the church, we (the brothers) cook the main dishes, while the ladies bring the deserts. Every now and then, my dad would help us cook. He was a deacon and he believed that men should have a strong presence in the home, the church, and the community. He felt that a man should lead by example and be willing to serve others. I can honestly say that I am a better man, husband, and father because of my daddy's example.

My daddy was a great man. He was a humble man, full of compassion, wisdom, and knowledge. He let me know that "People are destroyed for the lack of knowledge" (Hosea 4:6). He taught me to always include God in my decisions and to live by God's principles – His Word. The Word of God keeps a man rooted and grounded. My daddy always had words of encouragement to uplift and empower me to be the best that I could be. Although I didn't always want to hear these words, I knew deep in my heart that daddy was right. He was only trying to make me a better man. The lessons he taught me about love and forgiveness have made me a better human being.

In closing, my dad is no longer physically present with me here on earth. God saw fit to bring him to his heavenly home for some much needed rest and relaxation. He was a man of humility. He was a wonderful father to my brothers, my sisters, and me. He was a magnificent husband and friend to my mother. I love my dad and I know my dad loved me. In fact, he loved us – his family. We shared so many special moments together. These memories I will cherish and treasure for the rest of my life or until God calls me home. I will forever remember the lessons he taught me about being a man of integrity. Any man can father a child and become a father; however, it takes a real man to be a dad. Daddy, thank you for being a real man. Thank you for all your teachings, support, and love. I could not have made it this far without you. You will never be forgotten and your legacy will live on. I miss you and I love you. Mom loves and misses you, too.

A SPECIAL TRIBUTE TO LEO COLLINS, SR.: A REAL MAN

Alpha: May 05, 1920 – Omega: May 27, 1996

"Render therefore to all their dues: tribute to whom tribute is due; custom to whom custom; fear to whom fear; honor to whom honor" (Romans 13:7). In a day and age where divorce is at an all-time high, it's beautiful to witness a marriage that endured the storms of life and, yet, remained solid. When other men have decided to walk away from their marriage, like trading in an old car for a new improved model, and turn their backs on their children, I would like to pay a special tribute to a man who chose to honor his marriage vows and remain steadfast to his commitments. He made the conscience decision to stand tall in his home, church, and community. This is a special tribute to Leo Collins, Sr. – a real man.

Leo was born on May 5, 1920, in Amite, Louisiana. At the age of eighteen, he married the love of his life, Edwina Baker. Eleven months later, their first child was born. They named her Yvonne. There must be something special about the number eleven. I said that because eleven months after their daughter was born, they gave birth to a son. They named him, Leo Collins, Jr. Leo's family was now complete. He had just what he wanted – a wife, a daughter, and a son. Being a man, husband, and father, Leo went to work at a local foundry. Although he could neither read nor write, he refused to allow that to stand in the way of feeding and providing for his family. He knew that a real man didn't make excuses for his shortcomings. His wife and children could not eat excuses.

While attending Butler African Methodist Episcopal Church, Leo accepted the Lord as his personal Savior and became a born-again Christian.

It was his Christian faith that laid the foundation for his responsibilities as a man, husband, and father. He knew the difference between a churchgoer and a Christian. A churchgoer is a person who regularly attends church, but is not necessarily a Christian. A Christian is a person who attends church regularly, but is Christ-like – possesses the attributes of Christ. Leo, his wife and children all attended church together as a family. He believed in leading by example. Leo didn't send his family to church; he brought them with him. At Butler A.M.E. Church, he served faithfully as a steward, usher, and trustee. Leo had a charge to keep and a God to glorify.

In 1945, Leo met the next love of his life. He was hired to be the custodian at Amite High School. In the 1940s, Amite High was an all-white school. Desegregation was only a figment of someone's imagination. George Washington Carver once said, "There is just as much honor in tilling a field as there is in penning a poem." A real man takes pride in an honest day's work. Especially, when that job allows him to feed, shelter, and clothe his family. Leo loved his job and took great pride in a job done well. He once told me: "There is no shame in being a ditch digger. If you gon' dig ditches for a living, dig the best ditch you can."

As the school's custodian, Leo often had interaction with the student body. He always had kind and encouraging words for the students. They admired and looked up to him. It was kind of ironic. Leo never finished elementary school. Now he was going to high school each day. Not content with his inability to read and write, he made up his mind to change that. He began taking night classes at Amite High to learn to read and write. Although he never finished elementary school, he did learn to read and write. Kudos to you Leo!

Like most Americans, Leo wanted the American dream. He had a wife, a daughter, a son, and a good job. Now all he needed was a place to call home. Determined to provide the best life possible for his family, he purchased his first and only house. Love made it a home. Leo loved him some Edwina, and Edwina loved her some Leo. Together they raised their children in the fear of the Lord. They had pet names for each other. He called her "Doll" and she called him "Sweets." Theirs was a marriage made in heaven. They served each other with much love, respect, and admiration. When Edwina got sick and had to have surgery, Leo informed her that she didn't have to return to work. He told her that she could be a housewife, and he would go to work and provide for his family. As he went to work each day, he came home to a clean house, a home- cooked meal, two well-mannered kids, and a loving wife. Although Doll was a housewife, Leo was no stranger to the kitchen. He would often tell Doll to take a load off her feet while he cooked and helped out around the house. Anything Sweets could do to make Doll happy, he was able and willing to oblige. Doll loved making homemade cakes from scratch. She was famous for her homemade pound cake, which she made using her homemade butter. Sweets loved her pound cake. He was living the American dream.

The bible says, "A good name is rather to be chosen than great riches, and loving favor rather than silver and gold" (Proverbs 22:1). God gave Leo favor, but Leo earned a good name. He believed that a man's word was his bond. He paid all his bills on time and had A-1 credit. The only blemish he had on his credit was when he co-signed for family members and they failed to pay as they had agreed. In fact, I remember when he co-signed for my cousin to help her buy her first car. When the finance manager pulled his credit bureau, the salesman returned and said, "Mr. Collins, you can have whatever you want." Of course, my cousin drove off the lot with her new car. Leo knew the power of a good name – good credit. With a good name, you can get whatever your heart desires. I am reminded of a story I once heard about an old preacher and a young drug dealer. One day this old preacher overheard this young drug dealer bragging about all his material possessions. When the preacher heard all he could stomach, he approached the drug dealer and said: "Young man, you ain't nobody until you can walk into an establishment with no money and walk out with property just by signing your name." You can't buy a good name. You have to earn it!

As I bring this tribute to a close, Leo Collins, Sr. was my great uncle. He married my grandmother's sister – my mom's mother's sister. He was a wonderful husband and good friend to my great aunt Edwina. I respect him for being committed to his vow to love, honor, and cherish her and for being the husband of one wife. In May, 1996 (three weeks after his 76th birthday), he died of cancer. When he was first diagnosed, he informed the school system that he had cancer and needed to take an early retirement. After examining the records, it was discovered that he had accumulated five years worth of sick leave that he had never taken advantage of. Unlike most of us, my uncle's integrity would not allow him to call-in sick and take advantage of a sick day if he wasn't sick. Since he was now sick with cancer, the school advised him to take his sick leave. Once the five years worth of sick leave was exhausted, they would retire him.

What a mighty testimony! People came from everywhere to attend his funeral and to pay tribute to this law-abiding, decent, real man. His testimony was always, "May the life I live speak for me." His life spoke volumes at his funeral and is still speaking today. He was called "One of Amite's finest citizens." On August 4, 1999, the city of Amite held a memorial to honor my uncle. Following the memorial service, a dedication service was held with Amite's mayor, city officials, family and friends all in attendance. A section of South Street, where Leo lived, was renamed Leo Collins Sr. Street. At the dedication, a city councilman said, "Collins deserved this tribute. He was an example of respect and kindness to all who knew him." [*Amite Tangi Digest*, Wednesday, August 11, 1999] If I could have had a conversation with my uncle on his deathbed, I am confident he would have recited this passage of scripture: "For I am now ready to be offered, and the time of my departure is at hand. I have fought a good fight. I have finished my course. I have kept the faith: Henceforth, there is laid up for me a crown of righteousness, which the Lord, the righteous judge, shall give me at that day: and not to me only, but unto all them also that love his appearing" (2 Timothy 4:6-8). Rest in Peace, Uncle Leo. You were, indeed, a real man.

MY FAMILY: THE WIND BENEATH MY WINGS

Pick up any newspaper in any small town or big city, or turn on the television set and channel surf to the news broadcast of your choice and you will witness tragedy. Nowadays, tragedy is commonplace. Everywhere you turn and everywhere you look, you will see or hear something negative. To make matters even worse, family is plagued by tragedy as well. Divorce and domestic violence are escalating. Is there anything positive, inspirational, or uplifting to report? It appears that we live in a society that feeds off this type of news. On that note, I would like to share my story.

My name is Jay Atkins. I have been happily married for thirteen years. I have a beautiful, intelligent wife and four amazing kids – a twelve-year-old son, a ten-year-old daughter, a seven-year-old son, and a five-year-old daughter. I am an ordinary guy who possesses an extra ordinary love. I love my wife and kids – my family! They are my world – the air I breathe and the wind beneath my wings. Everything I do, I do for the welfare of my family. Family has always been my top priority. In fact, I can remember when I was in junior high school. One day one of my teachers turned and faced the class while he leaned on his desk and said, "Class, I want to ask y'all a question. Before you answer, take a few minutes to think about your answer. When you have your answer, be prepared to tell the class why you chose what you chose." As he scanned the room, he then said, "Y'all got that?" In unison we all said, "Yes, we got it." He then asked, "What do you want to be when you grow up?"

As you can imagine, excitement charged the atmosphere. Classrooms are more than platforms for learning and intellectual stimulation. They are also fields where dreams are fertilized. One by one, each student stood and told the class what he or she wanted to be when they grew up and why. There were the usual responses: a doctor, a nurse, a teacher, a lawyer, an actor, an actress, a rapper, a singer, an NBA basketball player, an NFL football player, an engineer, and so on and so forth. I was the last student to stand and proclaim my aspirations for the future. Can it get more dramatic than that? I stood up and said, "It really doesn't matter what I do for a living when I grow up. I want to be a husband and a father." When I made that statement, some of the kids started to chuckle and giggle. They thought I was trying to be funny. I was serious. Growing up without a father and never really having a real family, I have always wanted to be head of my own family. I wanted to experience the love of a wife and kids. I wanted to feel connected. There is no stronger connection than family.

When I was dating my wife, I had a conversation with an older Caucasian brother. We were just talking in general when he felt the urge to give me some advice. I am always open to receive good advice; therefore, I welcomed it with open arms. He said, "If you want to be happy in life, love your job and love your wife. When you love your job, you will enjoy waking up each morning and going to work. When you love your wife, you will love getting off from work and going home to be with your wife." When my wife and I got married, I was determined to put that into practice. There's not a day that passes that I don't show or tell her how much I love and appreciate her.

My wife and I are both employed. I am a mechanic and she is the head teller at a bank. Before we got married, we talked about family and how big of a family we wanted. We said we wanted four kids – two boys and two girls. We agreed that we wanted their ages to be close in proximity – about two years apart. When we got married, we touched and agreed on everything – we prayed. God answered our prayers and gave us just what we wanted – prayed for. After all, He said He would give us the desires of our heart.

If I get off work and arrive home before my wife, I shower and start dinner. When she gets off, she calls to let me know that she's on her way home and to see if I need her to pick up something from the grocery store. While she's en route, I start her bubble bath. When she arrives home, she gives me a hug and a kiss, takes her bath and changes into something more comfortable. She then comes into the kitchen and allows me to welcome her home properly with more hugs and kisses. After we get through telling each other how much we love and missed each other, she then sets the table, and jumps in to assist with dinner. If she gets off before me and makes it home first, the routine is the same. She takes her bubble bath, changes clothes, and starts dinner. I call her when I am on my way home. When I get home, I come into the kitchen and kiss and hug her and tell her how much I love and missed her. I then shower and change clothes. When I am done, I come into the kitchen and allow her to welcome me home properly. After we are done hugging and kissing, I then set the dinner table, and pitch in with dinner. While we are preparing dinner, we interact with the kids and inquire about homework assignments. Education is very important to us. We want our kids to be better and do better than us. My wife has an Associate's Degree in Accounting. When I graduated from high school, I enrolled in a trade school and studied auto mechanics. I graduated and received my certificate. I enjoy what I do because it allows me to provide for my family. We understand our role as parents. That's why education is a top priority for our children. There are many obstacles in life. A good education helps you to hurdle over a vast majority of them.

At dinner, we all gather around the table, grasp hands as a sign of unity, and we say grace. As the head of my family, I start the prayer of blessing. We then go around the table and allow everyone to say what they are thankful for. In my house, everyday is Thanksgiving – a day to be thankful. We don't take life for granted. We realize the fact that God didn't have to wake us up this morning, but He did. After grace, we take our seats and begin to feast. We want our children to have culture – know proper table manners and etiquette. Dinner is family time. It's a time where we bond as a family. At the dinner table, we have great conversation and discussion. No one is allowed to talk with his or her mouth full. We laugh, smile, and celebrate family. As a teenager, I only imagined moments such as these. Dinnertime is the highlight of my day.

After dinner, we clear the table, put up the leftovers, wash and put away the dishes, and tidy up the kitchen. In our home, we don't believe in going to bed and leaving a dirty kitchen. Once the kitchen is in order, we convene in the living room. We watch TV as a family, and we discuss everything we watch. Sometimes we let the kids watch television in their rooms if they choose. As I said, we discuss everything we watch as a family. The minds and thoughts of the youth are fascinating. We don't always agree on what program to watch; however, majority rules. One program that's not up for debate is the evening news. I think it is very important to know what is happening in and around the world. At bedtime, we hug and kiss each one of our kids and tell them that we love them. I think that it is crucial for my children to know that their daddy loves them immensely. My dad never told me that he loved me. I guess to him, it was a sign of weakness. Bedtime is daddy and mommy time. What goes on in our bedroom, as in Las Vegas, stays in our bedroom!

Neither my wife nor I work weekends. It wasn't always so. When we gained seniority on our jobs, we decided weekends were for family. Since the kids don't have school on the weekends, we believe it is vital that we devote this time to them. On Saturdays, we split up. I take the boys for boys' day out, and she takes the girls for some female bonding – girl time. It's important for me to bond with my sons. It's my job to mold, shape, and lead them into manhood. I want them to grow up to be men that any woman would be proud to bring home to meet her parents. I teach my boys to never disrespect a woman. For when they do, I tell them that they disrespect their mother. My sons love their mother. Our outing concludes with the three of us having dinner.

Sunday is Family Day. We attend church as a family. We believe that for the family that worships and prays together, its foundation is made that much stronger. After church, we partake in a family outing to have fun – catch a movie or go bowling. Later that evening, we have dinner at a local restaurant. We don't cook on the weekends. We work and cook Mondays through Fridays; therefore, weekends are set apart for family, fun, and relaxation. Since I spend Saturdays with my sons and my wife spends it with our daughters, On Sundays, I cater to my girls and my wife caters to the boys. It's important for my boys to know that their mother loves them equally as much as I do, and for my girls to know that their daddy loves them just as much as mommy does. We take pride in family.

Finally, we take a family vacation once every year. Before we had children, we celebrated our love for each other. We celebrated us. God smiled on me the day he blessed me to meet my wife. She is my soul mate and best friend. I love and honor her as both my wife and as the mother of my beautiful children. Each and every day, we rejoice and celebrate our love for each other and our love for our children. I can soar high because of the love of my family. My family is and will forever be the wind beneath my wings!

EVERYONE DESERVES
A SECOND CHANCE

Life is an adventurous journey that's full of potholes, roadblocks, side streets, one-ways, dead ends, forks in the road, crossroads and intersections, all which call for us to make choices on what direction or course we should take. Because of these perplexities, we don't always make the right choices. At times, life can be confusing. We all have days when the compass we call "judgment" gets cloudy and causes us to make wrong turns and go in the wrong direction – down the wrong road. Each of us has been forced to make a few U-turns in our lives. We are all human and prone to take wrong paths in life – make bad choices. Because humanity is what we all share in common, everyone deserves a second chance – everyone!

In the Gospel according to John, there is a story about a woman who made the bad choice of sleeping with a married man and was caught in the act. The Scribes and Pharisees (the woman's accusers) brought her before Jesus to be judged by the law. According to the Law of Moses, she should be put to death by way of stoning. Although it takes two to tango (commit adultery), they only brought the woman to judgment. While her accusers presented their case against her, Jesus was kneeling and writing on the ground. When her accusers finished laying out their case against her, they pressed Jesus to pronounce judgment. Jesus looked up and said, "He that is without sin, let him cast the first stone." Jesus continued to write on the ground. After Jesus uttered those words, the woman's accusers (all of them convicted by their own conscience) turned and walked away. When Jesus looked up again, it was just He and the woman left standing alone. Jesus turned to the woman and asked, "Where are thine accusers?" She replied, "I have none." Jesus then said, "Neither do I accuse you. Go and sin no more" (John 8:1- 11). In order words, Jesus said, "You are forgiven. Go home and don't do it again."

As a child, I was told that heaven has a record of everything we do and say here on earth. My grandmother used to say, "There's an angel looking and booking." What was Jesus writing on the ground while the men were accusing the woman of adultery? It is believed that Jesus was making his own case against the woman's accusers. Many believe Jesus was writing down the sins of each of the men that were standing in judgment of the woman; therefore, if any one of them would have picked up a stone to throw at the woman, Jesus would have exposed his sins to the crowd. Like the woman and her accusers, we are all guilty of making bad choices. Our fathers are not excluded. I am certain that if Jesus would have asked the woman why she chose to sleep with a married man, she would have given some lame excuse for her lack of better judgment. What amazes me is that Jesus didn't care what her excuse was, that's why he didn't ask her for one. Instead, he was more concerned about her soul. That is the reason he chose to give her a second chance.

When was the last time you took a moment and scrutinized your life – looked back over the choices you made? Are there some things you wish you could go back in time and have a do-over? Is there anything in your life you wish you could change? Be honest. We all have something in our lives that we wish we could re-do – be given a second chance to get it right. Some of our bad choices we made are there to teach us a valuable life lesson. When you learn from your poor choice, you should be a much stronger or better person.

Finally, "All have sinned and come short of the glory of God" (Romans 3:23). In a perfect world, no one would ever hunger or thirst, hurt or feel pain; fathers would love mothers and mothers would love fathers; families wouldn't experience domestic violence and be torn apart. As you and I both know, we don't live in a perfect world. Many of our fathers have wounded us and made us bitter against them. They have missed countless birthdays, holidays, sporting events, and graduations. The beauty of life is that broken hearts mend and wounds heal. Just as Jesus looked beyond the woman's faults and saw her needs, we must do the same thing for our fathers. If your father wants to be a part of your life, give him the opportunity to make up for lost time. As the saying goes, "Better late than never." It is never too late for a father to support his child. Although you may not be a child anymore, you can still benefit from spiritual, emotional, and financial support. If you have children, bring them into the equation. Wouldn't it be nice for your kids to experience the love of a grandfather? I wish my father was alive today. If he sincerely wanted a second chance to be my father, I would gladly give it to him. Everyone deserves a second chance! Chew on this thought for a moment. Be a role model for your father. Show him the face of a real man. Let him witness how a man is supposed to treat his family by observing how you interact with your kids. What do you have to lose?

A CAVEMAN'S MENTALITY

In March of 2006, I relocated back to the New Orleans area. I missed home and wanted to contribute to the rebuilding process. Nearly two months later, I started working for a security company as a security officer. About a month later, the company assigned me to work at a retail store that sold lumber products, building supplies, small and major appliances, household products, home furnishings, lawn and gardening supplies, products, and much more. When I received my orders, I was informed that I would be working five sixteen-hour shifts each week with a partner. Because I was used to working long hours, this didn't faze me. I loved overtime. Because of call-offs and no shows, I ended up working seven days a week. Many officers complained about the long sixteen-hour shifts. The company heard and answered their cries by converting the shift into two eight-hour shifts. When the company chose to go in this direction, I informed my supervisor that I wanted to work seven days a week. Since I was very reliable and dependable, he honored my request.

My partner was a nice-looking female officer. Although she was nice-looking, she was tough. We were assigned to patrol and maintain order in the lumberyard. We regulated and monitored the flow of traffic of customers picking up lumber materials. We also verified receipts for inventory control. Seeing that many residents were returning back to the city to begin the challenge of rebuilding, business was good – real good. I was popular with many of the customers. I was known as the singing security guard. Repeatedly, customers would tell me that I missed my calling. *Is any merry? Let him sing Psalms* (James 5:13). Each day that God allows me to wake up, witness, I count it a blessing. I sing in spite of Katrina. I sing because I'm still standing on top of the dirt.

Since I worked seven days a week, I became very familiar with the customers. Day in and day out, I would see the same customers – sometimes two and three times in one day. Many would say to me, "Damn, Shorty! Do you ever go home?" While others would say, "Shorty, you must live here. I see you every day." I would smile and say, "I can say the same thing about you. I see you everyday, too. At least I am making money, but you are spending money." They would laugh and play it off. I am a gregarious individual. I get along well with people. Because I saw some customers so regularly, I would say to them, "I better see you at the family reunion. I see you so much, it's like we family." They would respond, "No doubt." It didn't matter if they were Black, White, Hispanic, or Latino. Many felt like family.

My partner had her share of friendly customers, too. One morning this black male in his late 40s to early 50s greeted her. She smiled and spoke back to him. I was walking up as this exchange was in progress. My partner smiled at him and jokingly asked, "Why didn't you bring me any breakfast?" He looked her up and down before he responded. When he finished looking at her from head to toe and from toe to head, he said, "You are a woman. If you wanted breakfast, you should have gotten up early and cooked you some." I looked at him and asked, "What does her being a woman have to do with her being hungry and wanting breakfast? What's wrong with a man getting up and cooking him and his woman or wife some breakfast?" If you would have seen the expression on his face, you would have sworn that I had cursed him out or spoken in a foreign language.

He looked at me, with fury in his eyes, and said, "A woman's job is to cook my food and have my babies! Read your bible! You probably follow one of those women preachers!" He was very adamant and animated. I stood there and stared him down. It was very apparent that I didn't share his views. When he sensed this obvious fact, he questioned my manhood and walked inside the building. I stood there, held my peace, and watched him go inside the store. I held my peace and didn't offer my comments because I was at work and he was a customer. One thing I learned early in my Christian walk – you have to know how to pick your battles. In the words of Kenny Rogers (from his song, "The Gambler"): "You gotta know when to hold them, know when to fold them, know when to walk away, know when to run." If I would've gotten into a heated debate / discussion with this guy on a religious matter, I could've jeopardized my job; therefore, I waited until he went inside the store before my partner and I started laughing and conversing on what had just occurred.

This brief encounter left me wondering: How many men today have this same caveman mentality? If you see a woman that you like and find attractive, grab your club, hit her on the top of her forehead, grab her by her hair, drag her back to your cave, and force her to be your servant and love-slave. Each day you go out to fish and hunt for food, while the woman's job is to keep the cave clutter free, build a fire, cook your food, sex you up, have your babies, and speak only when she is spoken to. As your personal servant, the only opinion she is entitled to have is the one you give her. That's a caveman's mentality. Does this sound ludicrous to you? I sure hope so.

Brothers, we are living in the twenty-first century – the new millennium. Civilization has evolved and the days of living in caves are long gone. Caves have been replaced by fine homes; clubs and spears have been replaced by knives and guns; campfires have been replaced by elaborate ovens and stoves; horse drawn carts and wagons have been replaced by expensive and luxurious cars and trucks; and stay-at-home moms have been replaced by working mothers. In this twenty-first century that we live in, mothers are doctors, nurses, lawyers, engineers, accountants, teachers, professors, entrepreneurs, officers in the military, public officials, and the list goes on and on and on. Women are great movers and shakers in our time. Although motherhood is a woman's greatest calling, it's not her only calling. She is not a one-dimensional being. Women have mastered the art of multi-tasking.

These are changing times that we now live in. We must modify our attitudes – our ways of thinking– and adapt to the world around us if our families are going to survive. What many men fail to realize is that when a man marries a woman and says, *I Do*, what he is really saying is: *Today, I die to self and come alive to family. I'm trading in "I" and "Me" for "Us" and "We."* I like what Sister Souljah says at the end of her book, *The Coldest Winter Ever*: "When a man makes a choice to take a wife, he no longer belongs only to himself. He is in effect now promising to share himself completely. He is sharing not only his thoughts and moods, but his words and secrets, his challenges and struggles, his actions, reactions, and consequences, his finances and debts, his blessings and his sins." If couples don't crucify self and allow self to die, their marriage will be in a world of trouble. A real man puts the needs of his wife and children ahead of his own. Dr. King said in his autobiography (in reference to his father): "I have never experienced the feeling of not having the basic necessities of life. These things were always provided by a father who always put his family first." That's a real man!

According to Jennifer Baker of the Forest Institute of Professional Psychology (Springfield, Missouri), fifty percent of all first time marriages end in divorce. That's an alarming statistic. Why is the divorce rate so high and on a steady incline? Although I am not an expert, I would like to offer my hypothesis. It is my opinion that many couples have elaborate and expensive weddings but cheap marriages. The reason I call their marriages cheap is because they fail to invest in each other, building and enriching the life of their partner for whom they have vowed before God to love, honor, and respect. I am under the impression that many marriages are doomed to failure from the very start. Many couples enter into marriage with preconceived ideas and unrealistic expectations. The bible declares, "People are destroyed for the lack of knowledge" (Hosea 4:6). Ignorance is the lack of knowledge and the downfall of many marriages. I was taught: those who know better do better. It is a known fact that pre-marriage counseling helps reduce the risks of divorce.

Marriage is not a fairytale. It is a partnership that should be full of love, respect, teamwork, and concern for the health and well-being – mind, body, and spirit – of each partner. Believe it not, marriage is hard work. You don't instantly become "one" when you say "I Do." You must work at becoming one – one mind, one body, one soul. Each and every day of the marriage, both husband and wife must punch the clock – put in work. Unlike a regular nine-to-five job, marriage is twenty-four / seven. You can't take a break from your marriage. Every second you are away from the home, you are on call. Some days are easier than others and less stressful. Anything worth having is worth working for. Because many homes are two income families – homes where both parents work – men must help out around the house. After all, it's your home too! A dirty home is a reflection of every member of the household. If you don't know how to cook, clean, or do laundry, it's never too late to learn. Let your wife teach you the basics. This is a great opportunity for the two of you to bond and become even closer. You can teach an old dog some new tricks if he is teachable and willing to learn. Pro Football Hall of Fame member Emmitt Smith made this comment when he was a participant on *Dancing With The Stars*: "A real man will try to do something he can't do." Most men know how to cut grass and work on cars because they view these tasks as manly tasks, while housework – cooking and cleaning – is viewed as woman's work. That's a big misconception. A man who takes pride in his home and can manage / maintain it is more of a man in my eyes. Self-sufficiency raises the bar.

When I was in college, I shared an apartment with two other male students. Not long after I moved in, I discovered that one of my roommates had the bad habit (like so many other people) of letting dirty dishes pile up in the sink before washing them. When I come home from work, I have the tendency to stop in the kitchen first. If I see dirty dishes in the sink or a dirty countertop, I wash the dishes and wipe off the counter. When the roommate who left the mess in the kitchen returns home and discovers that I have cleaned up his mess, he confronts me and tells me that he was going to clean it up. I look at him and say, "I don't believe in procrastination. If you are going to do something, do it. Don't put it off until later, because later never comes." That's like the lady who said she was "going to pay" her energy bill when her lights got turned off, or the guy who said he was "going to pay" his car note when his car got repossessed.

Many nights I came home and found the kitchen in an uproar. When the guilty roommate returned to the scene of the crime, he and I had another brief discussion. I said to him, "As soon as you are done eating, you should wash out your plate or bowl and spoon or folk. It's much easier to wash one plate and one spoon than it is to wash a sink full of dirty dishes. It's just that simple! What's hard about that?"

He looked at me and said, "James, that's not how I was raised."

Were you raised in a barn? I thought to myself.

Many men have grown up in homes where their mothers did the cooking and their sisters washed the dishes. What happened to personal responsibility? If you drop it, shouldn't you be the one to pick it up? If you spill it, shouldn't you be the one to wipe it up? If you mess it up, shouldn't you be the one to clean it up? If you take it out, shouldn't you be the one to put it back in? If you open it, shouldn't you be the one to close it? If you break it, shouldn't you be the one to fix it or either take responsibility for breaking it? Shouldn't this be the message we teach our children – boys and girls? Is that too much to ask for?

Finally, when I was a teenager, my mother worked two jobs to raise her three sons – myself and my two brothers. My brothers were typical guys – they didn't like cleaning up behind themselves. Whenever they were hungry, they would get up and cook themselves something to eat; however, they would leave the kitchen in shambles. Many times, they would leave their dishes wherever they were when they ate. *I bet that sounds very familiar to a lot of people.* One day, I refused to clean up behind them. I decided to take a nap. While sleeping on the sofa, I heard a knock at the door. When I opened the door, I was surprised by a girl who came by to see me. Because I had refused to clean up behind my brothers, the house was dirty. I was so embarrassed! I told myself, *never again.* As I said earlier, a dirty home is a reflection of everyone who lives in that home. I can't lower my standards because the standards of those around me are low. To this day, I can't stand a dirty house or kitchen. I can't go to sleep with crumbs on the kitchen counter or dirty dishes in the sink.

In conclusion, a caveman's mentality is nothing more than a male chauvinistic attitude. This attitude will not be tolerated by women today. Women want to be pampered, not spoiled. They want to be treated like a queen. They want to feel blessed, safe, secure, and appreciated. It has been said that the way to a man's heart is through his stomach. Men love women who can cook. The same truth applies to women. Women love men who can cook just as much as men love women who can cook. As men, we must take the lead and lead our families to victory. We need to take pride in what's uniquely ours – our families. If you want to be treated like a king, treat your woman like a queen. Would you like to be a great man, a great husband, and a great father? If so, please allow me to tell you the secret to greatness. Jesus said, "If any man wants to be great among you, let him be servant to all." Serve your family – serve them a daily platter of love, security, and kindness. Be devoted to the happiness and welfare of your family. You reap what you sow. Your family will follow and serve you with eagerness and gratitude. Love your wife and support your children. It works. It really does!

THE THREE ROLES OF A FATHER: PRIEST, PROTECTOR, AND PROVIDER.

In the Old Testament, there is a story about a man named Job. It begins like this: "There was a man in the land of Uz, whose name was Job; and that man was perfect and upright, and one that feared God and eschewed evil. And there were born unto him seven sons and three daughters" (Job 1:1). Perfect? He was without spot, wrinkle, or blemish and had no pending scandals or skeletons hanging in his closet. Job feared God and he turned his face away from evil. He was a real man, a loving husband, and a devoted father. He understood and executed the three roles of a father: priest, protector, and provider. Let's examine these roles of a father – fatherhood.

According to Webster's Dictionary, a priest is "a person having authority to perform the sacred rites of a religion." A priest is also known as an "old man" or an "elder." Throughout this country, a lot of young men refer to their father as their *old man*. A father has the authority (power) to seek the face of God on behalf of his family. Why is it important to entreat the face of God on behalf of your family? The answer is quite simple. You seek the face of God for vision (direction) for your family, "For without a vision, the people perish." In other words, without insight or direction from God, your family will be destroyed or torn apart. Job realized this and he practiced it faithfully. Allow me to tell you how I know this to be certain.

Job's sons would periodically have feasts at their respective homes. When everything was prepared and in order, they would send for their sisters. Have you ever seen the movie, *Soul Food?* Well, Job's sons' gatherings were equivalent to Sunday dinners at the Josephs' house. They would fellowship – eat, drink, and be merry. After they had finished celebrating

– partying and getting their groove on as one might say – Job would send for his children. When they would arrive, He would sanctify them. The next morning he would get up at the break of dawn and offer burnt offerings unto the lord, according to how many children he had. Job said, "It may be that my sons have sinned and cursed God in their hearts" (Job 1:45). Do you know what your sons are doing when they are not in your presence? That's exactly why Job prayed for his family. He didn't and wouldn't leave anything to chance. He had God's favor and he wanted to make sure that his entire household was able bask in God's favor as well.

I have a Christian brother. He has three sons. His ex-wife – the boys' mother – would not allow the boys to go off to school, off to church, or out to play without first sanctifying them. Before they would leave the house, she would take a bottle of olive oil which had previously been consecrated, anoint each of their foreheads with a dab, and pray over each of them. Sometimes she would say, "In the name of Jesus" or "The blood of Jesus." I imagine Job laying his hands on each of his children just as she did with her sons. As a father, Job knew that as the head of his house, it was his responsibility to pray for his kids. Because he loved God and he loved his family, Job regularly prayed, sanctified, and offered burnt offerings on their behalf. When your children leave the place of refuge they call home, who knows who or what they will encounter in the streets, in the neighborhood, or on their school campus. As a father, you are the priest of your family and it's your responsibility to consecrate them.

Next, let's look at a father's role as the protector of his family. The famed psychoanalyst, Sigmund Freud, once said, "I cannot think of any need in childhood as strong as the need for a father's protection." I am smiling at this moment. Let me share the memory that has plastered this smile across my face. When I was in elementary school, I recall two boys having an altercation on the school playground. The smaller boy said to the bigger boy (who was a bully): "If you don't leave me alone, I'm gon' tell my daddy on you." The bully looked at him and said, "I don't care. Tell your daddy. My daddy is bigger than your daddy." That's how the mind of a child works. In his eyes, his daddy is superman. As long as his daddy is present, he's not afraid of the boogie-man. His daddy will protect him.

As a father, you are lord of your family. You are not the Lord of your family. That position is currently filled by Jesus; however, you are lord of your family. As lord of your family, you are the shepherd (guardian) and your family is your flock. As the shepherd, it is your responsibility to protect your family from dangers, seen and unseen. Your family depends on you for protection. Let's look at the life of a little shepherd boy named David. There was a day when a Philistine known as Goliath threatened the children of Israel. Because of his stature and threats, the children of Israel were afraid – very afraid. No man wanted to fight – go up against Goliath. Goliath was the biggest bully that had ever stepped foot on any playground.

One day the little shepherd boy came to visit his three brothers. David was the youngest of eight sons. His three oldest brothers followed King Saul and were away at camp. Jesse, their father, sent him to bring his brothers some lunch and also to check up on them – see how they were faring. While he was visiting his brothers, he heard the threats of Goliath. He also overheard some of King Saul's men talking about the reward that would be given to the man who would fight against Goliath and kill him. As David was inquiring about the prize for defeating Goliath, word got back to King Saul that someone was asking about the reward; therefore, the king sent for David.

When King Saul saw how small David was and that he was just a child, he told David that there was no way that he could challenge Goliath and win. This is a great life lesson. Never underestimate a man. You can't judge the magnitude of a man's heart – courage – just by looking at his stature. David looked the king in the eyes and said, "Thy servant kept his father's sheep, and there came a lion and a bear and took a lamb out of the flock: and I went out after him and delivered it out of his mouth:, and when he arose against me, I caught him and slew him (1 Samuel 17:34, 35). As the shepherd of his father's flock, it was David's job – responsibility – to protect the sheep from all impending danger. David didn't run from his responsibility. In fact, he welcomed it – ran towards it.

Allow me to digress for a minute and tell you about an event that happened when I was about thirteen years old. My great-grandmother (Mandy Baker) raised a few chickens. One day one of the hens strutted around the yard with a parade of biddies following close behind. I was so amused by this spectacle that I wanted to play with one of the biddies. As I ran behind the parade trying to pick up one of the biddies, I was attacked from behind by a rooster. I was about four feet, three inches tall, and weighed less than one hundred pounds. If you would have seen me fighting with this rooster, you would have laughed your head off. I almost peed on myself. When I was finally able to ward off the rooster, I realized that he was only protecting his family. That should be the instinct of every father. If someone breaks into your house and threatens the well-being of your family, it is your responsibility to protect them, even if it costs you your life. "Greater love hath no man than this, than a man lay down his life for his [*family*]" (John 15:13). I substituted the word "family" in place of "friends."

The last role of a father that I want to highlight and discuss is his role as a provider. According to Webster, a provider is "one who provides what is needed." I like that so much that I feel the need to repeat it. A provider is "one who provides what is needed." Many men have the delusion that child support is a monthly check that they send to their child's mother. Children need more than financial support. They need love, time, affection, spiritual guidance, discipline, and so much more. In fact, from time to time, they need simple things like hugs, piggy-back rides, and words of encouragement.

The bible says, "If anyone does not provide for his own, especially for those of his own house, he hath denied the faith and is worse than an infidel" (1Timothy 5:8). I am sorry. I have to keep it real. If a man won't provide for his own children, he is a fool! Children don't ask to come into this world. Children are the byproducts of having sex or making love. Even though there is a tremendous difference between the two, the end results are the same. I realize that some children are planned, while others are unwelcomed, unplanned, and unrehearsed. Regardless of how they were conceived, they have needs that must be met. As their father, they look to you to supply these needs. In his book, *The Audacity of Hope*, Barack Obama says: "I felt as well the mark that a father's absence can leave on a child. I determined that my father's irresponsibility toward his children, my stepfather's remoteness, and my grandfather's failures would become object lessons for me, and that my own children would have a father they could count on." If you are a man who can't answer the call of fatherhood, then you should learn how to "possess your vessel in sanctification and honor, not in the lust of concupiscence" (1Thessalonians 4:45). Because I just said a mouthful, I think I need to let you chew on that for a moment before you swallow so that you can better digest it.

In closing, the vast majority of the products we purchase come with an instruction manual. The manufacturer (creator of the product) wants us to get the optimal use out of what they have created for our convenience. Likewise, God is our manufacturer – creator. He, too, has supplied us with an instruction manual. The bible is our instruction manual for life as well as for fatherhood. There is so much we can learn and glean from the great men of the bible. "A fool despiseth his father's instruction, but he that regardeth reproof is prudent" (Proverbs 15:5). We can learn from the good and bad choices of others. That's why the bible is filled with both the triumphs and failures of men. No one plans to fail, but if you fail to plan, you will fail – won't succeed. There are statistics that say fifty-percent of all first time marriages end in divorce – they fail. When a marriage fails, children are damaged the most. Obama's aforementioned book makes this statement: "Sixty percent of all divorces involve children, thirty-four percent of children don't live with their biological father." So I ask each and every father, "What about the children?" What will become of them if you fail to be their priest, protector, and provider? Your sons are easy prey for ungodly predators. Do you care that your absence puts them in harm's way? Your lack of participation in your sons' lives puts stains on their souls. "The glory of children is their father" (Proverbs 17:6). Don't allow the devil to steal your son's glory. Your season of being missing in action is over. The time has come for you to report for active duty.

SUMMER
POEMS

A REAL MAN STANDS TALL

A good man obtaineth favor of the Lord…
Proverbs 12:2

God takes glory in a creature called man;
Made in His image – God's majestic plan.
Man should walk worthy with his head held high;
After all, he is the apple of God's eye.
"Made … lower than the angels," David said;
Honor and glory, God placed on man's head.

A freewill creature to choose as he please;
It's man's choice to or not to bend his knees.
Some have chosen to turn away from God;
Their hearts waxed cold and against Him made hard.
A real man will stand strong and will stand tall;
He is not ashamed to answer God's call.

A real man is no punk! Do you know what that is?
It's a man who won't stand for what's rightfully his!
And you thought it was a man who sleeps with a man;
It's really a man who's afraid to take a stand.
A real man will stand for all that is right and good;
He stands tall in his home, his church, and neighborhood.

For God he will live, and for God he will gladly die!
He accepts the truth: All men hurt and sometimes cry.

His wife and children respect and look up to him;
He works hard to provide a better life for them.
Today I ask, "Who will rise and answer God's call
To be a real man, standing strong and standing tall?"

ALL CRIED OUT

On a pillow of tears, I laid my head –
So many nights when I went to bed.
I wondered why you were never there
To show me that you really did care.
Each time I saw a boy playing with his dad,
I smiled even though my heart was sad.
When will you realize that I'm your seed?
Time, food, clothing, shelter is what I need.
Although my mother took you to court,
You failed to pay any child support.
This I could not grasp nor understand;
Even though you called yourself a man.
I am a man, but tears still often fall
When I look back to make sense of it all.
In spite of all the things you failed to do,
You are still my dad, and I don't hate you.
Death has come, knocking, to claim your soul;
The life you have lived has taken toll.
Lying in your casket so short and stout,
Sorry dad, no more tears! I'm all cried out!

THE DEATH OF A DREAM

When breath no longer fills the lungs within
When no place can be found to amend your sin
Flat on your back, arms crossed ... facing the sky
Spirit divorced body – farewell ... goodbye!

JUST THE TWO OF US

The day you were born, my whole world changed
You caused my life to be rearranged
In my arms, I held this tiny life
Would it be carefree or full of strife
As I held you, tears fell from my eyes
My love for you, I could not disguise
Responsibility, I embraced
Within you, innocence was incased
Through the night, I stood by your bedside
You filled my heart with such joy and pride
Your birth brought my life into focus
Against all odds, just the two of us

THE BIRTH OF RESPONSIBILITY

Today I became a real man,
When I watched you break through vagina's wall;
Today I became a real man,
So helpless … can't talk, walk, or even crawl.

Today I became a real man,
When I heard you exhale, burst into song;
Today I became a real man,
I embrace my place, know where I belong.

Today I became a real man,
When you fell asleep cradled in my arms;
Today I became a real man,
I surrender to your needs, to your charm.

A SPECIAL POEM FOR MOTHER

Boys will be boys: Isn't that what they say?
You can change that if you seek God and pray.
"Foolishness rests in the heart of a child;"
That's the real reason boys rebel – run wild.

Dad's not around: Don't use that lame excuse!
You are free from his physical abuse.
Teach your son respect for self and others…
Draw strength from church and neighborhood mothers.

Your love will be the wind beneath his wings;
All your praises, he shall forever sing.
Instruct him to be all that he can be;
Remember, your son is your legacy!

A FATHER'S ADVICE

Stand tall my son, like a redwood tree;
Be the man God ordained you to be.
Learn from my mistakes – poor choices in life;
Support your child, love, cherish your wife.
Work hard on your job, carve a good name;
Your branches will never sway in shame.

Stand tall my son, like a redwood tree;
Be the man God ordained you to be.
Life is a journey filled with choices;
Discern … decipher all the voices.
Your destiny is yours to command;
Power rests in the palm of you hand.

Stand tall my son, like a redwood tree;
Be the man God ordained you to be.
Do not let anyone define you;
To God and thyself, always be true;
When you possess the faith to believe,
Your goals, dreams, you will always achieve!

STAND TALL MY SON, LIKE A REDWOOD TREE;
BE THE MAN GOD ORDAINED YOU TO BE!

I'M SORRY

When we fail, we must confess
Heart attacks are caused by stress
Just because I was not there
Does not mean I did not care
You may never understand
Until you become a man
Grown-ups can be childish too
This is odd but still it's true
We don't always do what's best
Sometimes we won't pass the test
Look to God, He'll lead the way
Answers will come when **YOU** pray

THE PRAYER OF A YOUNG MAN

Lord, let me grow up to be a real man
To face life's challenges as best I can.
Let me know the depths of pain and sorrow;
Grant me hope for a brighter tomorrow.
Do not allow me to live in the past;
My faith and trust in *YOU*, let me holdfast.
When I'm hurt, give me a forgiving heart;
From my life, let not your Spirit depart.
Order my steps and guide me everyday;
I give up! I quit! Let me never say.
When I stumble … fall, grant me strength to rise;
When I am lost … confused, open up my eyes.

A CHILD'S PLEA

Dear Lord,
Thank you for waking me up
Thank you for giving me food to eat
Clothes to wear and a place to sleep

Lord, please bless mommy and daddy
They argue a lot and I don't know why
Mommy cries herself to sleep
Daddy is always angry

Lord, I love my mommy and daddy
Please keep my family together
I won't be bad no more
I promise! Amen

ARE YOU MY DAD?

I've dreamed of a man who looks like me;
I often wonder, who could he be?
Why doesn't he ever come around?
Does he live in a neighboring town?
Why don't mom ever talk about him?
Why aren't there any pictures of them?
Doesn't she know my life is not complete?
Will my father and I ever meet?
Can someone tell me: Was I a mistake?
Why don't I have a dad like my friend, Jake?
Now can you understand why I'm so sad?
Is it wrong for me to long for my dad?

Mom came to me with tears in her eyes;
What she told me took me by surprise!
She believes my father's name is Frank;
He was a donor at the sperm bank.
Single and childless, for this she was sad;
So, she made a lucky donor a dad.
I would have no dad like the av'rage kid;
She thought I may hate her for what she did.
Now my life may never be complete;
My father, I may never, ever meet.
For a mother's love, I am very glad;
But I'll always wonder: Are you my dad?

WHO WILL FEND FOR MICHAEL?

On the streets at night, he lays his head;
He longs for touch of pillow and bed.
Who will fend for Michael?

Two days ago, he turned seventeen;
God only knows the troubles he's seen.
Who will fend for Michael?

He steals to silence his stomach's growl;
Like jungle's lion, the streets he prowl.
Who will fend for Michael?

Trapped in a system he can't avoid,
A prison cell may be his reward.
Who will fend for Michael?

Tears drown the father he never had;
Thoughts of suicide don't seem so bad.
Who will fend for Michael?

Day-in, day-out, the story's the same;
An absent father gets all the blame.
Who will fend for Michael?

He lives in a world that's mean and cold;
Will Michael get the chance to grow old?
Who will fend for Michael?

Give Michael a fish, he'll eat today;
Teach Michael to fish, he'll eat each day.
Michael must fend for Michael!

A GIFT FROM GOD

Before sperm swam to egg to fertilize,
Before water broke and you opened your eyes,
I loved you.

Like a butterfly inside a cocoon,
You formed and grew inside your mother's womb
While love grew inside me.

My hand on her stomach to feel you kick;
Junior, you are my first draft – my first pick!
I love you.

From conception to birth, God and I talked;
Joy flooded my soul the day you first walked.
You are a gift from God!

SAFE IN MY ARMS

On my shoulder tears fall like drops of rain
The warmth of my embrace eases your pain
Cheek-to-cheek, I feel your temper'ture rise
My shoulder filters the tears from your eyes

Hush little baby ... don't worry ... don't cry
With each beat, my heart sings a lullaby
Like a sweet melody, it soothes your soul
In my arms, joy unspeakable I hold

Safety is in the cradle of my arms
They will shelter ... protect you from all harm
Like a shepherd attending to his sheep
In my arms, you are safe to fall asleep

YOU CAN'T KEEP A
REAL MAN DOWN

Out of the dust of the ground, God formed man;
Created in God's likeness: His master plan.
God called the first man, Adam, which means mankind;
A triune being – body, soul, and mind.

From Adam's ribs, God brought forth Eve – a helpmeet;
Enter woman – creation now complete.
Eve led Adam to eat from the tree of life;
Man disobeyed God and yielded to his wife.

Sin entered the world with death, its running mate;
Disobedience caused the grave to be man's fate.
"It is appointed unto man once to die";
Because of sin, man would bow his head and cry.

God sent another Adam to make things right;
The battle against sin, He would win this fight!
The world hated him! So, Him they crucified;
They nailed Him to a cross, pierced Him in his side.

"It is finished," were the last words He said;
"He gave up the ghost" then lowered His head.
They placed Him in a tomb – equal to the ground;
Christ showed the world: you can't keep a real man down!

Christ rose from the grave with power in his hands –
The power to heal and redeem fallen man.
Christ proved that He's the Life, the Truth, and the Way:
God knew that all men, like sheep, would often stray.

Like Adam, all men have sinned and fall short;
Only God knows the contents of a man's heart.
When you fall, dust yourself off and get back up;
Do not stay down and drink from sin's bitter cup!

Confess your weaknesses … stop being so hard;
Your son's respect may be your greatest reward!
How you start the race is not your story's end;
If you trip and fall, you can begin again!

STILL STANDING

Love and forgiveness are two keys to happiness
Cancerous is the heart that's filled with bitterness
A heart that's full of anger won't let love abide
Anger and bitterness are twins joined at the side

Life is too short to let dark clouds hide your blue skies
Don't build a house on a weak foundation of lies
Let truth be your cement, against all it will stand
A pillar of strength in a home stands a real man

Ev'ry man has his moment when his strength will fail
Hurt and disappointment fall from the sky like hail
Lessons can be learned in the classroom of defeat
Happy is the man who falls, but lands on his feet

FALL
LETTERS

THE BIG PICTURE:
A LETTER OF THANKS

Dear Dad,

I know this letter may come as a complete surprise; nonetheless, it is long overdue. For years I have longed to write you in hopes of getting answers to questions which plagued me as a child, teenager, and most of my adult life. But when I put pen to paper and started writing this letter, God flipped the script on me. The answers that I felt I was entitled to, no longer were important to me. God opened my eyes to see *The Big Picture*. Even though your rejection of me as your son hurt to the core, I know that I am accepted and loved by God. You can't begin to imagine the pain that is inflicted upon a boy when he learns that his biological father denies paternity. Because of your rejection, I am an introvert – I keep my feelings and emotions buried deep within me, hidden from everyone. Both pride and arrogance shield my tears, while my inner man weeps beyond the shadows.

For years I have felt like a victim, walking around with my head hung low, feeling sorry for myself because of your lack of interest in the matters of my life. But thanks be to God who gives us the victory. One Sunday morning as my pastor was preaching, God spoke through him and said, "Lift up your head, O you gates! And be lifted up, ye everlasting doors! And the King of glory shall come in" (Psalms 24:7). When I stopped feeling sorry for myself and raised my bowed head and allowed the King of glory to come in, I realized that in Him there are no victims. Victors! Not victims. I know God has a purpose for my life. Even though you, my biological father, deny that I am your son, I have a heavenly father who will never leave, forsake, nor deny me. You may not want to believe this, but you have helped me to become the man that I am today. And for that I want to say, "Thank you."

Many people say that experience is the best teacher. I firmly believe that. Well, if that is a true statement, then inexperience is a lesson well learned. The reason I say that is because I learned how to be a father to my son by looking at the things you never did for me. I embrace the fact that my son is my legacy, my heritage. Therefore, I will never inflict pain on him by denying the fact that he is my son. In fact, he is my pride and joy. So is my daughter. But since I am dealing with the father-son theme, I'll stick to the subject at hand. My son will have lasting memories of me because you never gave me any of you. He can lay his head down each and every night knowing that his father loves him, because I cried myself to sleep many nights and went to bed each night without the blanket of a father's love. Because of my pain, my son will never experience the pain of not having his father as a part of his life.

When he needs a hug, I will be there to hold him. When he gets out of line at home or at school, I will be there to scold him. When he is discouraged, I will be there to encourage him. When he feels weak and wants to give up and throw in the towel, I will be there to strengthen him. When he stumbles and falls, I will be there to pick him up. When he is afraid and scared, I will be there to hold his hand, to protect him. When he does well in school, on the basketball court, baseball or football field, I will be there to applaud and cheer him on. I will be there to guide him through the stages of boyhood, all the way through to manhood. You see, the reason I am here for my son is because you were never there for me. Unlike you, I love and honor my son by being in his life. So as you can see, you helped to make me the man and father that I am today. What you have taught me, I could not have learned in college. So that I won't be viewed as an ungrateful son, dad, I must thank you for helping me to see *The Big Picture*. Thank you, dad, for everything! "And we know that all things work together for good to them that love God, to those who are the called according to his purpose" (Romans 8:28).

Yours truly,
Your son

A LETTER TO THE GRAVE

Dear Dad,

Recently, I ran into a Christian brother of mine. He is a pastor at a church here in New Orleans. In times past, we have had lengthy discussions about my relationship with you. As we talked, he sensed that I still had some unresolved issues with you. He suggested that I write you a letter with my left hand. He knew I was right-handed; therefore, I gave him a strange look. He pleaded with me to comply. I gathered that writing the letter with my left hand was a psychological gesture that would reveal something buried deep within my psyche. At the time, I refused to comply. As the days and weeks progressed, I reflected on that conversation. After much thought, I came to the conclusion that writing you a letter may give me a sense of solace and closure. Seeing that I am right-handed, I chose to write the letter using that hand.

Before your death, I visited you in the hospital. You were in a coma, clinging on to life as best you knew how. I arrived when other family members had ended their visit and were leaving to go home. I came at the right time because I needed to be alone with you. At first, I was speechless! But as I stared at you knocking on death's door, I realized that this may be my last chance to speak my mind. You were a hard man to talk to. You always dominate the conversation and over-talk anyone trying to get a word in edgewise. This was my time to talk and your time to listen. Even though you were in a coma, I believed that my spirit would connect with your spirit, and you would know that I was there by your side when you needed me the most. I rubbed your forehead and sang you a Gospel hymn. Do you recall that visit? I believe you heard every word I said. I am writing you this letter because I have a lot of unanswered questions and things that I have to get off my chest. I believe this letter will be therapeutic.

Growing up as a child, I was often taunted because I favored you. As you know, Jerry and Mooney are light-skinned like our mother, while my complexion is dark like yours. As a result of my darker complexion than my brothers, I was often called *Blacky*. Consequently, I grew up with an inferiority complex, thinking being light-skinned was better than being of a darker complexion. I felt that lighter complexion Blacks fared more favorably in society than their darker complexion counterparts. I bet you weren't aware that I was teased. Were you? Well, I was. Don't sweat it! I grew out of it. I learned to love me for me. After all, God loves me.

Dad, there are a few things that I need you to help me understand. One day you were slapping mama around on Grandma Mandy's porch. Grandma yelled out your name several times and pleaded with you to stop beating her daughter. When you wouldn't stop, she approached you. You turned around and punched her in the eye. Dad, you hit her so hard that she went soaring off the porch (dad, I kid you not) like a character out of a *Batman* comic book. Why did you hit Grandma? Why didn't you stop beating my mama – the mother of your sons? How could she defend herself against you? She was only four-foot-eleven and weighed about 130 pounds!

What about the time when the two of you were arguing and she asked you to leave? I know you remember that day. You left, but returned the next day. While mama was at work and we were at school, you pulled up to the house in your 18-wheeler truck and loaded it up with all the furniture in the house and then left. Let me fill in the blanks for you. When we returned home from school, we were all stunned to see an empty house. Mama knew that you were responsible. You always had a bad habit of thinking only of yourself. How could you do something so low? That night, I cried myself to sleep as I slept on that hardwood floor. I now realize that the marriage was irreconcilable. You were selfish and pigheaded. All you had to worry about was yourself. Mama had to raise three boys by herself. It was evident that you didn't give a damn.

When we woke up the next morning, mama let us know that the Lord would make a way for us. Personally, I didn't see how. The Lord was in heaven. He didn't sleep on that hard floor last night. I believe mama knew that I was affected the most by what you did, seeing that I was more sensitive than my brothers. Crying was not a hard task where I was concerned. I guess, in a way, I was a bit of a crybaby. Had you been around more often, you probably would have given me something to cry for. Do you remember that time when I ran home from school because a boy at school wanted to fight me? If you don't, I do! You told me that you would whip my butt (that's not the word you used) if I didn't go back and fight him. I was more afraid of you than I was of him. Because I didn't want a whuppin' from you, I went back and beat him up. I guess in your own way, you were trying to teach me that a real man doesn't run away from a fight. Let me get back to what I was saying before I digressed.

While we were at school, mama went down to Louisiana Furniture Store and bore open her heart to the store manager. In case you have forgotten, mama possesses the type of faith that can move mountains. Once again, we were stunned when we returned home from school. This time, mama stunned us. We walked into a house filled with new furniture. Mama was right! The Lord had made a way; however, that wasn't the only thing that was new. Mama had procured a second job to help pay for all the new furniture. Just in case you have forgotten or don't know, mama is an amazing woman! As they say, "One monkey don't stop no show!"

Now on to something more intimate. I want to tell you about a movie I saw starring Denzel Washington entitled, *Courage Under Fire*. The movie had a profound effect on me. After the movie was over and as I was driving home in my car, I became overwhelmed with remorse and had to pull over to the shoulder of the interstate. I could not hold back the tears. Would you like to know what triggered this outpouring of tears? I'll tell you anyway. The movie was about a female officer (who was a mother of a little girl) who died in the line of duty. She sacrificed her life to protect her men – her family. Even though she had a daughter back home who she dearly loved, she made the ultimate sacrifice. Her mission was to lead her men to accomplish their assignment. It was her responsibility and duty to protect the men that followed her leadership. She did not take this responsibility lightly. Why didn't you make any sacrifices for us – your family? You were our father. Couldn't you make some sacrifices for us? Mom did!

Dad, I have another question that demands an answer from you. Why didn't you pay child support? It was evident that you despised mama for divorcing you. What about us? Did you despise us also? What did we do to you? How could you despise me – James Jr.? I am the spitting image of you. Did you even care whether or not we lived or died? If you had any concern for our well-being, I couldn't tell. There were many nights I went to bed hungry. I cried myself to sleep, hoping food stamp day would hurry up and come. As you can see, I made it through those dismal nights – no thanks to you. My bad! I am sorry. That was my flesh acting up.

We were blessed to have a mother who was a good seamstress. We didn't wear a lot of name brand clothes; however, we were always neat and clean. Mama made most of our clothes. A single mom raising and caring for three boys without financial or emotional support from their father isn't an easy feat to accomplish. Despite that fact, mom did it! All things are possible with God's help. I guess you weren't aware of that fact. As I look back, we wouldn't have had to struggle if you would have been a real man and honored your vows and taken care of your responsibilities to your family. We could have fared nicely and lived pretty comfortably. You were not hurting for money. I saw a few of your check stubs. Driving trucks is a lucrative profession. I better leave that one alone. There's no need for crying over spilled milk.

Approximately a week after my visit to you in the hospital, I was almost killed. What a coincidence! You and I both hospitalized at the same time. While crossing the street on my way to work, I was struck by a speeding car. The car ran a red light and struck me, then fled the scene of the accident. God spared my life. However, I underwent surgery for two fractured bones in my left leg. The next evening following my surgery, I was discharged and sent home on crutches. The accident occurred on Wednesday, December 22, 1999. I spent Christmas alone, while you were alone in the hospital in a coma. I hope you were making peace with God. The realization of my circumstances slapped me dead in the face. I could not hold back the tears from cascading from my eyes. I am blessed to be alive to write you this letter.

Three weeks after my accident, I received word that you had passed away. Dad, if I may be frank with you, in my heart you were already dead. Because of this truth, I was remorseless when I heard of your passing. You died on your birthday. How ironic is that! I attended your funeral on crutches. The main reason for my attendance was because I didn't want the backlash from my uncles, aunts, and cousins on your side of the family. I had deduced that they would have reached the conclusion that my hatred for you wouldn't allow me to attend your funeral. I was recuperating from an auto accident; therefore, I had a good reason to be excused. To keep down confusion, I chose to come to your funeral and pay my respects.

It was a nice service. Many people had some wonderful things to say about you. I had to look at the program to make sure that I was at the right funeral. I didn't have such fond memories of you as the people speaking at your funeral. I must admit, I felt sorry for you. I hoped you had gotten your affairs straight with the Lord. If you hadn't, it is too late to do it now. There was nothing I could say or do that would be beneficial to you now. Since I had long considered you dead, I had no more tears to shed on your behalf. I realize that may seem kind of harsh, but it is the truth. It took a lot of tears and years for me to have arrived at that destination; therefore, I refused to allow you to hurt me again.

I have to wrap this letter up. I am mature enough to know that everything happens for a reason. Although I didn't cry at your funeral, I cried weeks later. Unhealed wounds later caused me to breakdown. Dad, I want you to know that I have finally found peace. I have accepted the reality that your absence helped me to discover my destiny. For that, I must say, "Thank you." I framed your program and placed it on the stand which holds my television in my living room. Whenever I'm in my living room, I glimpse at your picture. It is the first and only picture of you I possess. Why I framed your obituary and placed it in my living room, God only knows the answer to that question. Perhaps, it is my way of having you near me each day – my way of keeping you close to me. Finally, I have never heard you say these words to me; therefore, I will tell them to you now. In spite of everything, I love you. Rest in peace!

Your loving son,
James Jr.

AN ANSWERED PRAYER:
A LETTER TO MY SON

Dear Junior,

I heard of some men referring to their child as an accident or mistake. They said that they never planned on being a father so soon. For the record, I want you to know that you were never an accident or a mistake. You are an answered prayer. Before you were ever conceived, I held and played with you in my dreams. I rocked and sang you to sleep. I changed your dirty diapers and played with your belly while you looked on and smiled. Many nights, I prayed and asked God to bless me with a son. I told God that if He would grant my prayer and give me a son, I would nurture him in love and respect for his fellow man. I promised God that I would raise my son to be a man of honor, respect, and decency. Son, you are my answered prayer!

Junior, you are my responsibility. I don't take responsibility lightly. I will teach you how to be a real man by walking upright before you and by the way I treat others. I will teach you how to be a good husband by the way I treat your mother. You will never witness me hitting or beating your mother, and you will never see or hear of me disrespecting her in any way. I will teach you how to be a loving father by the way I treat you. I will always have time for you. I will teach you how to be a good provider by going to work each day, by returning home each evening, by paying the bills each month when they are due, and by keeping food in your mouth, clothes on your back, and a roof over your head. As long as you are a child, you will never have to worry about paying rent or bills. You will never go to bed hungry or be naked or destitute. This is my promise to you, my son. Most men don't realize that a child is more than just a responsibility. Caring for and raising a child is a ministry. God has placed you in my life for me to shepherd you into manhood.

Finally, the bible says, "A wise son maketh a glad father" (Proverbs 10:1), but "A foolish son is grief to his father" (Proverbs 17:25). Junior, you are a wise son. You have never disappointed me. Your teachers are very fond of you, and you have never brought home a bad report. You are almost as good-looking as your old man – almost! I am very proud of you, and there is no doubt in my mind that you will grow up to be nothing but a strong (real) man. Before I end this letter, I must reiterate: you are an answered prayer. I thank God every morning I am allowed to open my eyes, get out of my bed, and breathe His precious air, for sending you into my life. In all honesty, you are the best part of me. You are one of my greatest blessings, and I love you.

Love,
Dad

HIGHLY ESTEEMED: A LETTER TO THE MOTHER OF MY SON

Dear Sweetheart,

I know what you are thinking. You think that I want something from you. It's been a long time since I called you *sweetheart*. In the past, I have called you many things, but *sweetheart* wasn't one of them. When tempers flare, we are both guilty of doing and saying things that, later, we both regret. Before I go any further, I want to apologize for my behavior and attitude. For all the hurt, pain, and sorrow that I have caused you over the years, I apologize. I pray that you can find the generosity within your heart to forgive me. Indeed, I am sorry.

The reason I am writing you is because an evolution has begun in my life. Simply put, I have grown up and seen the light. Finally! I matured and have become a man – a real man. I have surrendered my life to God and asked Him to take control of my life. He has opened my eyes to see the things which ignorance and immaturity blinded me from seeing. One of the things God has shown me is what a wonderful woman and mother you are. Although you didn't create our son by yourself, you managed to raise him by yourself – without any financial, emotional, or spiritual support from me. You have done a wonderful job raising our son. He is a respectable, responsible, and mature young man. This is a byproduct of some good home training. You did good. Real good!

I want you to know that I have written our son and offered him an explanation as to why I was on the sideline and wasn't an active player in his life. Please know that I didn't give him a bunch of excuses because there is no excuse that would suffice for a father to not be in his son's life. I humbled myself and told him the truth. I went as far as telling him about how excited you were when you discovered that you were pregnant with him. In hindsight, I realize that the reason I ran from my responsibility was because, simply put, I wasn't a man. A real man will not run from his responsibilities. I asked for his forgiveness and I also asked him if I could be a part of his life. Whatever role he would allow me to play, I will gladly accept. I just want to be a part of his life.

To make a long story short, I have the utmost respect for you as a woman and as a mother. I am grateful that you didn't shun your responsibility like I did. I am also grateful that you ignored my immature comments and didn't abort the pregnancy. I now realize that a man doesn't have the right to demand that a woman have an abortion. That's your body, and you – you alone – must make that decision. I realize that with that procedure comes much baggage – physical, psychological, and spiritual scars. If I wasn't ready for a child, I should have worn a raincoat. To prove to both you and our son that I have grown up, I have enclosed a check for most of the back child support that I owe you. In the upcoming months, I will send you the remaining balance. I am fully aware that this check doesn't change the fact that I wasn't there for you or our son, but I hope it will serve as a catalyst to a great friendship between us. Once again, I want to thank you for taking great care of our son. For a job well done, I highly esteem and applaud you.

Yours truly,
Your Baby Daddy

A NEW BEGINNING:
A LETTER OF APOLOGY

Dear Son,

First, I want to say that there is no excuse for me not being a part of your life. Although I don't have an excuse, I do owe you both an explanation and an apology for my absence. It's my prayer that after you have read this letter, you will find space in your heart to forgive a fool like me and allow me an opportunity to build a relationship with you.

Hmmm ... where exactly should I start? Let me start from the beginning when you were conceived. When your mother first told me that she was pregnant with you, I was both scared and angry. I thought to myself *how in the hell did I get myself into this predicament*! I felt that I was too young to be a father. Not only did I think that I was too young, I knew I wasn't ready to be a father. If the truth were told, I had some more *wild oats* to sow. Being a father is an awesome responsibility. I was having a hard time trying to be a man. I couldn't bear the thought of becoming a father. In fact, I didn't know how to be a father. My dad left my mom when she was pregnant with me. Being the independent woman that her father and mother raised her to be, she raised me by herself. Of course, her mother (my grandmother) helped as much as she could. My dad was a sorry excuse for a man. Unknowingly, I was walking in my father's footsteps. I guess it's true: *Like father, like son.*

When your mother learned that she was pregnant with you, she was so happy. If you would have seen her, you would have sworn that she had won the lottery. The thought of becoming a mother brought her so much joy. When she came to me and told me that she was pregnant, I told her that I wasn't ready to be a father. She looked at me and said, "Ready or not,

I'm pregnant." She quickly let me know that I didn't have a choice in the matter. In eight months, you would be born. Because I was immature and hardheaded, I wanted to prove to her that I did have a choice concerning my life. No one was going to make me be a father. I wasn't ready. I had more growing up to do.

That's enough about the past. I am sure you get the picture. Since I can't change the past, I won't dwell on it or try to relive it. Son, I have matured and realized my deficiencies. I am no longer that boy who thought he was a man. I am a man – a real man! I have turned my life over to God and asked Him to guide my life down the path He wants me to take. In me surrendering to God, I vowed to be responsible and abide by His Word. I attend church on a regular basis, and I have a good job which pays me a decent salary. I am not rich, but I ain't poor either.

Son, I have confessed my failures of fatherhood to God, and I believe in my heart that He has forgiven me. My pastor preaches that God is the God of second chances. Son, I am confessing my failures to you and asking for your forgiveness. I know that as your father, I have been a big disappointment to you; therefore, I would like to rewrite a few chapters in your life so that your story and mine's may have a happier ending. I know that I can't change the past or undo what has been done; however, wounds can heal and broken hearts can mend. I really would like the opportunity to build a relationship with you as your friend. When you feel that the timing is right and that I am worthy, I would like to be your father. I am your father in theory (biologically); however, I want to be your father in deed and in truth. I know that actions speak louder than words. To show my sincerity, I have written your mother and enclosed within that letter a check for most of the child support that I am in arrears. In the upcoming months, I will mail her another check for the remaining balance. I realize that my life is not complete without you being a part of it. I hope this letter and gesture (check that I sent to your mother) will be the first step towards a new beginning for the two of us. Son, I love you! Do you realize, that's the first time I have ever said those words to you?

Please forgive me,
Your Father

REGENERATED: A NEW LEASE ON LIFE

To Whom It May Concern:

Winston Churchill once said, "Man comes into this world armed only with his mind." This may be true; however, as he grows and matures, he discovers that he must arm himself with more than just his mind if he plans on surviving in this world. I learned this foundational truth at an early age. Due to the lack of a positive male role model in my life, I turned to the streets for guidance and emotional support. I studied long and hard and received my degree at the *School of Hard Knocks*. I majored in hustling!

The streets taught me to get it how I lived. It also taught me to rebel against and resent authority. By so doing, I would be tough – hard. One of the greatest lessons the streets taught me was to never allow anyone to punk – disrespect me. When I reached a certain age, I was very ornery. Not even my mother could control me or tell me what to do. Because I had to get it how I lived, I felt that I was *a grown-ass-man*! As a man, I was determined to be *king of my castle*. My castle was synonymous to my life. I had to protect and get me by any means necessary. I owe that to Malcolm X.

As a man, I believed that every woman wanted a piece of me. Because I was tall, built, dark and sexy as hell, I knew that I was God's gift to women. I felt that I could have any woman I wanted, and I did. I owed it to them to spread myself around, to sow my wild oats, one might say. I craved the attention that women gave me; however, I refused to be on *lockdown*. Stick and move was my philosophy. If I had a condom, I used it. If opportunity presented itself and a condom wasn't within reach, I went with the flow – basked in the moment. You only live once, right? Because of this lackadaisical attitude, I unknowingly impregnated my *li'l shorty*. To keep it real, when she told me that she was pregnant, I was looking forward to having a li'l man to kick it with. Yeah, I was hoping it would be a boy.

A few months after Shorty told me that she was pregnant, I was arrested for selling drugs to an undercover narcotics agent. When I went to court, I was found guilty and sentenced to five years in prison. In the past, I have had several brushes with the law and spent a few nights in jail, but nothing of this magnitude. As the old saying goes, "If you make your bed hard, you have to lie in it." That's what my mother always said whenever I wouldn't listen. I had no other choice but to lie in the bed that I had made for myself.

One day while in solitary confinement because of a physical confrontation with another inmate, I received a letter from Shorty. She wrote me to congratulate me on being the father of a healthy baby boy – seven pounds and six ounces. Wow! I was a father. For a brief moment, I paused and pondered my new status – a father. Since I was all alone, I allowed tears to pitter-patter down my cheeks. The fact that my son was born while I was incarcerated opened my eyes to reality. If I didn't modify my present course, lifestyle, my son would grow up without a father like I had. I hated my father for not being in my life. I guess that's the reason why I was so rebellious and destructive. To tell the truth, I blame him for everything that has gone wrong in my life. I couldn't bear the reality that my son would grow up without me in his life and that he might hate me as a result of my absence.

When I was released back into the general prison population, an evolution had begun in my life. A fistfight was a daily occurrence in prison. There were many guys in the joint who bragged about the fact that they had killed someone on the outside. It became very apparent to me that prison is full of not only hard criminals and hustlers, but killers as well. I busted a few heads in my day, but I never took a man's life. I beat some up pretty bad, but at least they lived to fight again another day. As I took a panoramic view of my surroundings, I knew that it was time for a change. My fellow inmates may not have a reason to live, but I do! My reason weighed seven pounds and six ounces!

While attending chapel service a few weeks later, the evolution reached a new level. We had a guest speaker who made a big impact on my life with his testimony. He was an ex-convict who reformed himself in prison. While in prison, he obtained his GED and completed several college correspondence courses. Upon his release from prison, he enrolled in a nearby community college and earned his Associate's Degree. He concluded his testimony with the following statement: "The bible says, 'The race is not given to the swift neither is the battle given to the strong but unto him that endures unto the end.' In other words, it's not how a man starts a race, but how he finishes the race that counts." He went on to say, "It ain't over 'til it's over. Never count a man out because he is down. Just because you are knocked down doesn't mean that you are knocked out! You can't change your past, but you can modify your future by the choices you make today. It's true, a leopard can't change his spots, but men change every day. Just because your father was in jail or was on drugs or was an alcoholic and wasn't present in your life, doesn't mean that you can't be successful. You control your destiny. God can and will break generational curses. You can stay down and have a pity party or you can get up and rise above your circumstances. The choice is yours."

I left that service with great expectations about my present and future. I convinced myself that if he could do it, so could I. So could I! I remembered when I was a child, I heard a preacher say, "God is not a respecter of persons. What He has done for others, He will do for you." With that in mind, I signed up for GED classes. In less than a year, I received my GED. I became a role model inmate. I was determined to be a man my son could and would be proud to call *daddy*. I gave my life to God and allowed him to create in me a clean heart and renew a right spirit within me. I knew that I couldn't make it on the outside without God at the helm of my life. Before God could do a work in my life, I had to forgive my father of all his sins against me. I believe God allowed me to get sent to prison in order to save my life from a violent death in the streets. I now realize that you have to go through in order to get to – come out!

In conclusion, I would not recommend prison to my worse enemy. You can go in hard and come out even harder. Going to jail or prison doesn't validate your manhood. If the truth be told, it negates it. Going to jail or prison means that you made some bad choices in your life. Prison is a form of slavery. We were born to be free. Freedom is our birthright. It's only by the Grace of God that any of us can leave prison alive and a changed person. You don't get many second chances in life. When you are blessed with a second chance to right your wrongs, you must make the best of it and put your best foot forward. I am up for parole in a few months. If it is God's will, I will be paroled. If not, let the evolution continue. I can't wait to hold my son for the first time. I want to be a man that my mom, my son, and even I can be proud of. I hope that this testimony will inspire someone to give God a chance. You have tried everything else. Try God. I am glad I did. I gave Him a chance and He gave me a new lease on life!

Forever Grateful,
A New Creature

AN EARNEST APPEAL:
A LETTER TO MY DAD

Dear Dad,

I am writing you this letter because I don't know if I have the heart or the courage to tell you these things in person. I hope you don't think that I am soft or a sissy because I'm writing you this letter. I believe that it is time for you to know what's in my heart. I will sleep better at night, knowing I found the strength to write you and tell you what was on my chest.

As a small child, there were many nights that I cried myself to sleep. I always wondered: *Where you were, what you were doing, if you were okay, and if I would ever see you again.* Each time I visit my friends and see them playing, laughing, and joking with their dads, I envy them. Although I would be smiling on the outside, thunderous rain would be pouring inside. Sometimes I try to be tough, but it's not easy all the time. When I see how eager their fathers are to make sure that they enjoy life, I can only imagine how good that must feel.

Dad, I am at that age where a boy really needs his father. Don't get me wrong, mom is wonderful! She's always there for me and has taught me so many valuable life lessons; however, she can't teach me to be a man. That's your job. I don't hate you for not being a part of my life, at least right now I don't. I feel that my life would be so much better if you came around more often and spent more time with me.

Dad, I am appealing to your heart. Think back to when you were a kid. Maybe your dad wasn't a part of your life. If that was the case, how did that make you feel? You probably felt the way I am feeling at this present moment. Whether or not you choose to be a part of my life, you will always be my dad and I will always be your son. Nothing and no one can change that. The only thing that may change is whether or not I still love you. And dad, I don't want to hate you. Cross my heart and hope to die. I don't!

Love,

Your Son

A HUSBAND'S PLEA

Dear God:

I know it's been awhile since you and I have talked, but I really need your help. I need divine intervention. I'm gonna keep it real with you. I have to. You are God. You know what I'm gonna do or say before I even *do it* or *say it*. I'm about to be exposed for sticking my hand in the cookie jar. I cheated on my wife and now this "bi- - -". ... I'm sorry. I forgot who I was talking to. The woman I had the affair with is threatening to tell my wife everything if I stop seeing her. When I told her that I wanted to end our affair because I was tired of sneaking around and lying to my wife, she told me that I better handle my business and keep satisfying her if I want to save my marriage. In the beginning, it was exciting. It felt good that a woman, other than my wife, wanted me. I felt alive again, like I still had "it." Whatever "it" is! Because of my stupidity, I'm about to lose *it* – my marriage that is. How could I be so weak and foolish?

God, I love my wife and my son. I can't let this crazy bi- - -. Damn! I keep forgetting that I'm talking to you. I'm sorry. I'm frustrated and angry with myself for being so weak. It's not her fault. She didn't cheat on my wife. I did! I made the vow to love, cherish, and honor my wife, not her. I can't lie to you. You are God. You know the contents of my heart. This is my first and last affair. I violated my wife and destroyed her faith and trust in me as a man. She doesn't deserve this, and I don't deserve her. She is a good woman, a great wife, and a wonderful mother. My cheating had nothing to do with her. It was all about me and my ego. I was thinking with the wrong head. Tonight I plan to be a real man and *bite the bullet* and tell her everything. She deserves to hear it from me – the man she married and loves. I'm sorry for being a weak man, God. Please forgive me of my sins against you, my wife, and my mistress (that's not the word I want to use but you know, God). I am a man and I should know better. I love my wife and my son and I will do whatever it takes to salvage my marriage and keep my family together. God, please give my wife an understanding and forgiving heart when I tell her tonight. This is my plea. I ask this in the name of your son, Jesus.

KEEPING IT REAL:
MY SIDE OF THE STORY

Son, it was good seeing you last weekend. Based on our conversation, it is clear to me that you are bitter and haven't forgiven me for walking out on you and your mom when you were a child. You have to understand the fact that things were different back then, and I wasn't the man that I am today. Don't get me wrong, I'm still not perfect. There's always room for growth, improvement. I haven't reached the end of my journey. You asked me some questions that I wasn't prepared to answer at the time. You caught me off guard. I always knew the day would come when I would have to give you an explanation as to why I wasn't there for you – face the music – as my mother would always say. However, I wasn't expecting that day to be this past weekend. Since then, I have been doing a lot of thinking – soul searching. You are no longer a kid, and I think it is time that you learn the truth. I am going to keep it real with you because you deserve to know the real reason I wasn't a part of your life, growing up.

Before I proceed, I want you to know that just because I wasn't there when you were growing up doesn't mean that I didn't care about you and your well-being. I chose the path with the least resistance. I knew there would be some fallout; but I could deal with that at a later date. Before you were born, your mother and I were having problems. I'm not going to lie to you or sugarcoat the truth. Back in the day, your pops was a *playa*. Like most guys, I enjoyed the company of women. I loved them – big ones, small ones, thick ones, slim ones, tall ones, short ones. It didn't matter. I didn't discriminate. They were my weakness. I was a dog, and your mother knew this. I never understood why she thought that she could change me.

Let me hip you to the game, son. Can't no woman change no man unless he wants to change.

Your mother was crazy about me. She couldn't stand the thought of seeing me with another woman. She was possessive as hell. I'm not bragging when I say this. Your mother was sprung. I honestly believe that she got pregnant on purpose hoping that having my child would force me to settle down and be the family man that she wanted me to be. Her plan worked for a brief moment; however, she became a hemorrhoid. Think about it. Where are hemorrhoids found and what do they cause? I told you that I was going to keep it real with you.

Day in and day out, she would nag and fuss about this and that. Somewhere in the bible it talks about how it is better for a man to be on the top of the roof than inside a house with a nagging woman. Don't think that I am blaming your mother for everything that went wrong in our relationship. I have to share some of the blame. I wasn't completely innocent. However, your mother knew that I wasn't ready to settle down. Instead of her letting nature take its course, she tried to manipulate fate. A woman shouldn't try to play God and change a man. Your mother knew how I was when she met me. Change doesn't happen overnight or come easy. There are some things a man has to go through – experience – before he can wake up and smell the coffee.

After you were born, I tried to make it work with your mom and me and be a family man. She wanted us to get married. I wasn't feeling that. We were having too many problems. Just because we had a son together, that wasn't a good reason for us to get married. Marriage wouldn't magically make our problems disappear. In fact, I honestly believe that if we would have gotten married, our problems would have gone from bad to worse. Your birth didn't stop her nagging and our arguing. Neither did it stop my eyes from roaming. I want you to know that I did care about your mother. However, she didn't complete – totally satisfy me. I couldn't quite put my finger on it, but something was missing in our relationship.

One day your mom and I got into a very heated argument. I am not proud of what I am about to tell you. That particular day, your mom pushed the wrong button. Before I knew what happened, I snapped and hit her. Although she provoked me, there's no reason to justify a man putting his hands on a woman, especially the mother of his child. I should have walked away and allowed myself some space to cool-off – calm down. Although I was sorry for hitting her, that didn't change the fact that I hit her. At that moment, I knew she wasn't the woman for me. Any woman that can provoke a man to hit her is toxic. Armed with this realization, I told your mother that it was over. I honestly felt that she was too toxic for me. I could not endure the constant nagging and fussing. As I was leaving, your mother gave me an ear full – told me where to get off!

Days later, when she realized that it was indeed over, she told me she was going to put me on child support. She said that she would make sure that no other woman would get all my money. I told her that I was cool with that. I never denied the fact that you were my son. Just because she and I didn't get along didn't void my responsibility to you. Therefore when the child support papers arrived by certified mail, I signed them and paid what I was assessed by the courts and moved on with my life. As time passed, I met a new woman who really complemented me nicely. I grew to love her. She was the total opposite of your mother. She was good for and to me. I told her all about you, and she (we) wanted you to be a part of our lives. When your mother saw us together, I told her that we wanted to spend time with you. She looked at my new woman and told me that if I wanted to spend time with you I had to promise not to bring you around my female friends. I don't think it is necessary to repeat the words she used to describe my female companions. I won't insult your intelligence. You are fully aware of the words she used to describe my female friends. Once again, she was trying to control (run) my life. I didn't have a problem with her bringing you around her male friends. Therefore, I didn't understand why she had a problem with you being in the presence of my new girlfriend or any woman I chose to keep company with. She was just being vindictive, as usual. That's why I got out when I did.

To make a long story short, every time your mother and I would occupy the same room, she would find some way to start an argument. That was irritating as hell! Spending time with you meant putting up with your mother and having to hear her mouth. Life is too short to have to deal with all that drama, day in and day out. That's why I made the decision to be a silent partner in your life. Although I missed significant years in your life, I never missed a child support payment or failed to pay any increase. I felt that when you became a man, you could decide whether or not you wanted me to be a part of your life. I always knew that the day would come when I would get a chance to tell you my side of the story. It doesn't matter what lies your mother fed you over the years about me. I know the truth. I didn't turn my back on you. I ended my relationship with your mother, not you. You have always been in my heart, thoughts, and prayers. I believe that everything happens for a reason. When you were a kid, I wasn't a role model for you or any boy. I'll never know what your life or my life may have been like if I would have been a part of your life and allowed you the opportunity to be a part of mine. I can't change the past – unscramble eggs; but I can right my wrongs. I want to be a part of your life and I want you to be a part of mine. Who am I kidding? I'm not getting any younger. I need to be a part of your life, and I need you to be a part of mine! Life is too short to be estranged from your family. You are my flesh and blood. You are my legacy. I look forward to that day when you will make me a grandfather. I don't want you to choose the same path I chose. I want better for you. You deserve better.

In closing, I hope that after hearing my side of the story, it sheds some light on the shadows of your childhood – helps you to better understand why I chose to be on the sideline in your life. I now realize that my absence has caused you great pain, frustration, and anxiety. For that, I am deeply sorry. I am only human. We all have shortcomings and make bad choices. No one is perfect. We don't always choose the right paths in life. Believe it or not, we grow from our wrong choices. What doesn't destroy us only makes us that much stronger. We can have a strong father-son relationship if you make the choice to allow me to be a part of your life. God knows that I want to amend my sins towards you. But know this: I am a man under construction. God is not through with me yet!

Your Father

TO MY READERS

Thank you for investing your money and time in my ministry – buying and reading my book. I hope you were **M**otivated, **U**plifted, **I**nspired, and **E**ncouraged by what you read. Although I am an adult, I do not consider myself to be grown; perhaps physically, but not spiritually, mentally, emotionally, or intellectually. Each and every day of my life, I am growing – learning. I welcome your comments, suggestions, opinions, as well as your constructive criticisms. "Whoso loveth instructions loveth knowledge, but he that hateth reproof is brutish" (Proverbs 12:1). My ears are always open to listen and hear. Please email your comments to the following email address: <u>livingepistlespublishers2@yahoo.com</u>. I love hearing from my readers. Always remember, nothing is too hard for God. Because we are children of God, we can do all things through Christ who gives us the strength to be successful. Once again, thank you for your patronage and support.

James A. Harrell, Jr. (kjdapoet)